What Others Are Saying

It is a rare and precious thing when a gifted and successful leader takes the time to pass their collected wisdom on to others in written form. When that leader has achieved success on three continents across multiple professional disciplines such as medicine, ministry and business, the book they create becomes invaluable. *What I Wish I'd Learned* is such a book. Kola Alao's compelling narrative informs the mind and ignites the heart. By integrating proven leadership principles, compelling personal anecdotes, and timeless spiritual truths, Dr. Alao inspires the reader to greater levels of self-awareness and a passion for personal achievement.

John Carter
Lead pastor, Abundant Life Christian Center
Syracuse, New York

What I Wish I'd Learned by Dr. Kola Alao is an exceptional book with writing that is brilliant, straight-forward, honest, and so very human. A remarkable combination of profound wisdom *and* a quick read. It is simplified in short, clear chapters (not a boring lecture) that make the point with great impact. Weaving in Dr. Alao's personal story (both good and bad) and clinical vignettes makes it compelling. Finally, I like the direct advice he gives—too often we give the pros and cons but do not take a stance. Even when people may disagree with him, he will have earned their respect!

Mantosh Dewan, MD
President, SUNY distinguished service professor
Upstate Medical University, Syracuse, New York

I want to start by thanking Professor Alao for writing this book. *What I Wish I'd Learned* is a treasure, a service to mankind. It is filled with wisdom for the ages garnered through relatable personal experiences and presented in easily digestible language. It is also an easy and fun read, a book you return to every now and again, not just to refresh your memory about the nuggets embedded in it, but also to tap into the hopefulness the book engenders in readers. It is clear Professor Alao put much thought, effort, and care into giving us tools for a better life, and I believe it will generate as much excitement for anyone who reads it—young or old, professionals or non-professionals alike—as it has done for your lucky physician residents and medical students.

Charles C Dike, MD.
Professor of psychiatry and co-director, law and psychiatry division
Yale University School of Medicine

At last, Kola (as we know Dr. Alao) has put into writing what we as friends and colleagues have witnessed firsthand! His vast knowledge of human psychology, expertise in mental health, and survival skills successfully traversing life in three different continents is something to greatly admire. This book, *What I Wish I'd Learned,* gives a wonderful insight into Dr Alao's strategies for dealing with issues at different stages of life that can serve as a useful guide. He has interspersed this book with snippets of his faith, life experiences, and psychology to provide an understanding on how one can manage the different challenges of life. Knowing Kola and his wonderful wife, Lola, as a couple over many decades, there is no doubt a lot of the inspiration for the writing of this book as Kola mentions would have come from Lola's prayerful encouragement and prompting to the great heights they have achieved together to the admiration of many.

Tongue in cheek, the one thing missing is Kola's foray into Surgery and Radiology early on in his career and how he found his natural home as a widely respected and knowledgeable psychiatrist! Kudos Kola for giving us an insight into all your success and how you did it. Information that many can learn from and put to practice.

Kunle Ashaye
Consultant psychiatrist, visiting professor
United Kingdom

What I Wish I'd Learned is truly an insightful and transformative read. Dr. Alao has crafted a remarkable masterpiece that goes deep into powerful and practical principles, presenting them in a way that is both accessible and enlightening. The S.M.A.R.T. goals framework and the principles of change resonated profoundly with me, offering actionable steps that anyone can apply to achieve growth and transformation in their lives.

What sets this book apart for me is its subtle yet profound foundation in biblical truths. I believe this unique approach makes the content relatable to both believers and nonbelievers alike, inviting everyone to explore the timeless truths of successful living.

Dr. Alao encourages readers to reflect on their own journeys and the changes they wish to implement. I am genuinely looking forward to diving deeper into the pages of this book, as I believe it will offer guidance and encouragement for anyone seeking to navigate the complexities of life. Thank you, Dr. Alao, for sharing this invaluable work with the world; it is a guide for transformation, hope, and purpose!

Lee Wilson
Lee Wilson Ministries

What I
WISH
I'd Learned

Practical Tips for Living
a Fulfilling Life

Dr. Kola Alao, MD

What I Wish I'd Learned: Practical Tips for Living a Fulfilling Life
Copyright © 2024 by Dr. Kola Alao, MD

Unless otherwise noted, all Scripture quotations are from the *Holy Bible,* New Living Translation, copyright © ©1996, 2004, 2007, 2013, 2015 by Tyndale House Foundation. Used by permission of Tyndale House Publishers Inc., Carol Stream, Illinois 60188. All rights reserved.

Scripture quotations marked (ESV) are taken from the ESV® Bible (The Holy Bible, English Standard Version®). ESV® Text Edition: 2016. Copyright © 2001 by Crossway, a publishing ministry of Good News Publishers. The ESV® text has been reproduced in cooperation with and by permission of Good News Publishers. Unauthorized reproduction of this publication is prohibited. All rights reserved.

Editors: Annette Hogan and Angela Fae.

ISBNs: 979-8-9905297-0-0 (Paperback)

979-8-9905297-2-4 (Hardcover)

979-8-9905297-1-7 (Ebook)

Printed in the United States of America.

10 9 8 7 6 5 4 3 2 1

Dedications

I dedicate this book to my beautiful, loving wife, Lola.

Your support and sacrifice over the years is the reason I am a successful man today.

To my son Dami and my daughter Katelyn.

Thank you for encouraging me to push myself further than I thought possible.

To my lovely daughter, Dey, thank you for believing in me more than I believe in myself.

Acknowledgments

I would like to thank and recognize God for loving me more than I understand and giving me what I don't deserve.

I would also like to acknowledge my Pastor, John Carter. Thank you for the emotional and spiritual support over the years. Many of the ideas in this book were inspired by your preaching, teaching, and training. Thank you, Pastor John.

Lastly, I would also like to thank those who have helped me along the way. You have accepted me as I am, flaws and all, and still chosen to support and love me anyway.

Contents

Preface

Education teaches us to receive, memorize, study, and sometimes apply book knowledge, but there are many lessons in life that escape even the best students. Unfortunately, I was one of them. As a well-educated man, I still had to learn the subtly social, furtive financial, opaque political lessons of life the inconvenient way. Through trial and error, I took notice of my successes and my mistakes. Over the years, I have paused and analyzed how I responded to conflicts, procrastination, communication, negotiations, self-care, anger, finances, etc. Then, I questioned what other options I had. As similar situations arose, I became better at navigating the best options for me and my family. As I did so, the outcomes improved. Life became easier and this made me happier.

I share this same life advice with all my resident physicians and medical students. They are constantly shocked by the simple but easily applicable lessons that improve their life, ease their stress, and just make them plain old happy. So passionate about what they learn, they have carried my lessons into their classrooms and shared with others. As a result, I've been invited to speak and give lectures about "life after medical school" at various universities. Students regularly approach me afterward, thanking me for opening their eyes on how to avoid life's hardships. At later points in their life, my protégés have texted and emailed me explaining how they have applied my strategies to their life. They exclaim their excitement about quickly paying off their mortgages, saving money, getting better interest rates, negotiating better deals on cars, spending quality time with their family, and more. They express feeling safe and at peace. It has been their surprising and overwhelming gratitude and reception of these ideas which inspired me to write this book.

But, lucky you! I have organized and explained all my practical life lessons here in this book. If you feel so compelled, now you can change your life and live it to the fullest too.

Section 1

Personal Development

Chapter 1: Change

We have all been there: the clock strikes midnight, the New Year starts, and we make a resolution. This resolution is a pledge or commitment to make a change in your life. Many people like to make New Year's resolutions, whether to start exercising, stop drinking, quit smoking, or commit to a relationship. However, about ninety percent of people who make New Year's resolutions quit within the first three months.

Why does this happen so frequently? As you might have experienced yourself, making these changes is difficult. There are forces working against you when you try to create change in your life. These forces exist even though the only thing that is guaranteed in our lives is change. An additional complication is that change is intimidating and sometimes perceived as "for the better" and sometimes "for the worse." Since change is inevitable and the only constant in life, *we need to change in order to thrive in life*. If one is resistant to change, it leads to stagnation and lack of progress.

In this chapter, we will discuss the forces that oppose us when we are trying to make a change and provide practical approaches for how to make effective and lasting ones.

There are two types of change.

Intentional Change: This is what we typically think of when we want to make a change. It is a conscious decision. For example, a person may decide to stop smoking because they read an article associating smoking with cancer. They want to change their habit and, by force of will, quit smoking in order to prevent a cancerous outcome.

Crisis-driven Change: This type of change happens when outside, impending, and typically negative events are the catalyst for the change. Let's assume the person described above did *not* quit smoking and eventually developed lung cancer. Now they *need* to quit smoking. The change has become necessary. This change is the result of the impending crisis.

I strongly recommend making intentional changes rather than waiting for a crisis to do it.

Resistance to Change

It is important to understand *why* change is difficult. Resistance to change can stem from circumstances, environment, people, and ideas (or mindsets).

- Circumstances in your life may make it difficult to change. For example, if you are working hard to pay off debt, it might be difficult to have time for the gym, even though you want to increase the amount of exercise you are getting.
- People who are close to you may oppose your change, either consciously or unconsciously. For example, it is not uncommon that when two people are in a relationship, if one partner decides to lose weight, the other partner may subconsciously start cooking unhealthy meals, making it more difficult for their partner to change. Change is easier when you are with like-minded people.
- Ideas and mindsets can also cause resistance to change. We all have preconceived notions about what is normal and what is not normal. These ideas might affect our ability to desire change. For example, physicians who are stuck in the old idea of using pen and paper may find everything wrong with electronic medical records.

Once we recognize that there are obstacles to making changes, it becomes important to have strategies in place that help us move past these barriers. These strategies help us anticipate the unanticipated, expect the unexpected, and lastly, get us ready to stand against the forces that resist change. It is important to recognize what you can change and what you cannot change.

Forces Against Change

We need to be familiar with the forces against change in our lives. In addition to the resistance to change, there are three laws of physics that work against you when you want to make a change as well.

The Law of Inertia

The law of inertia, Newton's first law of motion, states that an object at rest remains at rest unless it is acted upon by an outside force, and an object in motion continues to be in motion, in a straight line and at a constant speed. In recognizing this law, consider which forces get you to move and which forces stop you. For example, if you want to exercise, identify what it will take to get you up and out to the gym. So, if you want to stop a bad habit like smoking, determine the force that will interrupt your success. Consider the law of inertia. What prevents you from overcoming the resistance to change? Giving yourself space for this thought process will help you decide what it will take for you to change. Identifying that ahead of time will help you prepare to overcome it.

The Law of Force and Acceleration

Newton's second law of motion describes the relationship between force and acceleration. If you increase the force on an object, the acceleration increases by the same factor. To put this more simply, once you have decided to make changes, there will be forces propelling you in a particular direction. There will also be forces preventing and dissuading you from changing direction.

Anticipate the forces against you. You may be hesitant to get outside your comfort zone. For example, a few years ago, I was on a weight loss program that included reduced food intake and weekly exercise goals. After losing forty pounds, my weight loss stalled. After doing some research, I realized that I needed to accelerate my exercise. I had been walking on the treadmill for an hour, so I started a high intensity interval training (HIIT) program. If you aren't familiar with HIIT, you perform a series of exercises to a timed interval. You do as many push-ups or weight lifts as possible during the interval, then move on to the next exercise station. This is fun and also increases your metabolism. By doing this, I moved out of the comfort zone of performing the same exercises in the same way and started to lose weight again. It is important to anticipate the forces that stall or accelerate your progress. And while going through these changes, you need to create strategies to overcome them.

The Law of Entropy

Newton didn't only explore optics and motion. He also studied thermodynamics. Newton's second law of thermodynamics is often referred to as entropy. It states that everything tends towards chaos, becoming more disorganized. If you don't take care of something, the natural tendency will be for it to become disorganized. Your health, weight, wardrobe, hairstyle, the cleanliness of your house, and so on are all excellent examples. Without intention, things degenerate. It requires conscious effort to anticipate how this law works against the change you want.

What will help you make a successful change?

First of all, don't give up! You can guarantee that the moment you try to make a change there will be forces working to prevent it: internal forces, external forces, and extraneous forces. If you anticipate them, you can develop strategies that will help you succeed.

Why should you change?

If you don't change, you may become obsolete. For example, the Eastman Kodak Company was the most successful camera and film company in the world, but it resisted digital technology and suffered great business losses. The phrase "you can't teach an old dog new tricks" is not a good phrase to live by. We must learn new tricks and ways of being—and that means we must be willing to change over the course of our lives. Change is also an important aspect of personal development.

In the next illustration, you will see four circles which are called the circles of control or circles of change. Take notice that the only circle that you have full control over is the one in the very center.

The Circles of Control

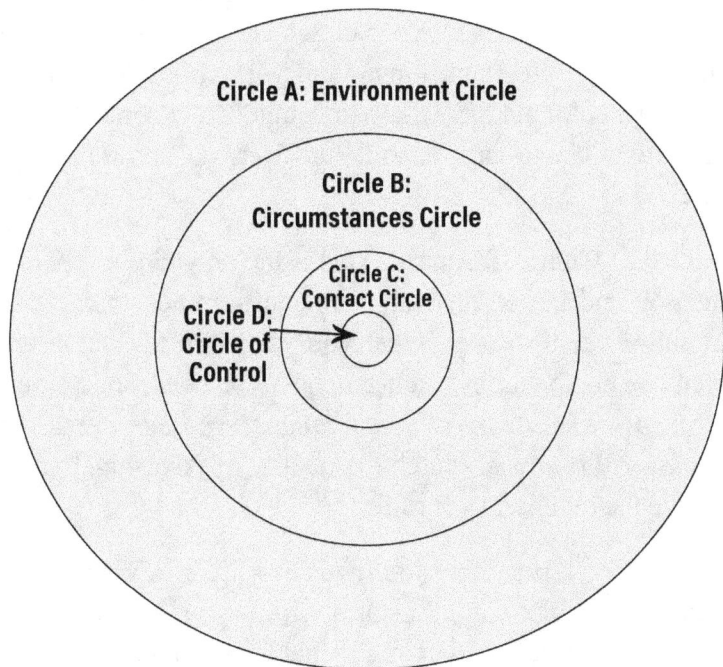

Circle A: The Environment Circle. This circle represents things that happen in the larger world. Examples include the tsunami in Southeast Asia, a shooting incident in El Paso, Texas, or any other environmental factor or event, such as snowstorms, floods, or any other local ecological challenges. These are completely outside our control, and recognizing this will save you from wasting time. These environmental and cultural circumstances affect us directly and can be traumatizing.

Circle B: The Circumstances Circle. These are external circumstances that occur closer to home. These also cannot be changed or directly controlled by any individual. These include happenings just outside our sphere of influence that still affect us in our daily life. This may include something like a local shooting, a car accident, or a robbery.

Circle C: The Contact Circle. Most people find this circle to be the most difficult. The circle of contact includes people you meet at work (especially that coworker who drives you crazy), your family members (including your in-laws), your friends, your classmates, even your children. You may be able to control certain things with your children before they turn six or seven years old, but after that you cannot fully control them. We all desire to control others to some extent, but we cannot and *should not* follow this impulse.

Circle D: The Circle of Control. This is the only circle we *can* control. This is internal and has to do with your ideas, mindsets, and behaviors. You can control what you eat, what you watch on television and social media, what you do, to whom you listen, how you react, and yes, even your thoughts. *Since you can control your thoughts, you can eventually determine the course of your life.* Watch the quality of your thinking because it will determine the quality in your life.

Ultimately, if you prioritize and focus on Circle D, your circle of control, change is possible. Change starts within you. Furthermore, if you are aware of "the resistance to change" that encompass your life and "the forces against change" that will impede your decisions, you are more likely to be successful because you know to expect delays and bumps along the way. However, you cannot let these interruptions trump your desire to change. Once you have successfully changed the flaws within your own circle, then you can proceed to address issues in the outer circles: circles C, B, and A.

The following steps will help you undertake these necessary and liberating changes in your life. It may help to write or journal your thoughts as you work through the following list.

Steps for Change

Develop clarity about the change you want. Identify your goal for the change. Why are you changing?

Be specific. Use visualization and your tactile senses to imagine how you will feel and what you will do after making the change. In our example of losing weight, how would losing weight impact your life? What will it feel like at your next medical exam, during your next clothes shopping trip, when hiking up a mountain, or running during your next game of tennis?

Invite others into your process. This is a way of aligning yourself with like-minded people and it helps build accountability. Enlist support from friends, family, coworkers, or a support group. Surround yourself with people who know you. People who are able to speak to you truthfully and honestly are a great help. Set up regular contact. If you utilize the services of a coach or other paid advisor, make sure they really want to aid your success. The important thing is to tap into godly and appropriate counsel while committing yourself to honesty and transparency in your relationships at the same time.

Recognize that change is not easy. There are forces gathered for resistance. Opposition may come from your family or social set and, most importantly, from your own unconscious assumptions. For example, while you're trying to lose weight, you are invited to a family member's home and offered high-calorie options, such as fried food. Now, you are tempted to be a polite guest and go against the boundaries you set for yourself. You are now on the verge of dismantling your goals. What are your own hidden agreements that form barriers to change? Are your own ideas about what is comfortable stopping you? Or do you doubt your own ability to change?

Make a plan. Set S.M.A.R.T. goals: Specific, Measurable, Attainable, Relevant, and Time-based. Look at the big picture. To do this in our example of weight loss, you may plan your schedule at the gym, talk to potential walking partners, listen to informative podcasts, and get advice from people who have been successful in meeting a similar goal. See more on this in the next chapter.

Anticipate distractions. You may have to set boundaries in order to make changes in your life. Take time to think about habits, people, and environmental factors that may divert your attention from your new plan. For example, if you work in a stressful environment and may miss meals, think ahead and carry healthy snacks and water with you to work rather than face the temptation of eating from the vending machine or getting takeout.

If you want to start journaling every day, consider the possible distractions as well as how to fit it into your schedule. For example, when you sit at your desk, is there a tendency to put other tasks first, such as paying the bills or answering emails or playing a game? Are you spending more time making coffee than journaling? Distractions like these can derail your writing plans. In other words, set time aside for the process of change, so you can successfully incorporate new tasks and mindsets into your daily life.

Take set action steps. This is when you start to execute the change. You have made a plan, and now you can break it into several action steps and start taking these steps. Be decisive and keep going. If you are working on your physical fitness, take the action step of regularly walking or running uphill during your workout. If your goal is weight loss, determine how often you will weigh yourself on a scale, and stick to the plan. In this way, you can translate your vision for change into specific, small steps that build toward your goal of changing a behavior or attitude.

Be courageous. Disconnect from doubt and fear. It's important to push through discomfort when making changes. If your body is aching from the workout, be sure to use those sore muscles the next day, too. If your goal is to cook more vegetables, don't be discouraged by new flavors. Keep going. If you want to play guitar, keep practicing, and don't be discouraged. The sounds emerging now will help you gain experience with the instrument, so you can make music. Exercise patience and stay strong; you will be surprised by just how much you can do.

Develop discipline by pushing hard. Recognize that small setbacks are part of the process. Get comfortable with discomfort. You actually learn more about the process and the type of change you are making through setbacks. If you do the same workout every week, you will probably plateau in terms of fitness and weight. Once you learn to alter the workout and incorporate new moves and disciplines, you will be proceeding to your goals. Making progress in other areas is similar. If you don't write in your journal for a couple of days, you may find that you miss it. In this way, you can discover more about the goodness of the change, why you are making it, and what it is truly doing for you and your well-being.

Celebrate the wins. All of them, not just the big milestones. As you set action steps in place for your overall plan, take regular time for reflection. Allow yourself to recognize and savor the progress you've made: how the body is stronger, how many pages were written, how many more vegetables have become part of your repertoire. Don't let hidden, negative mindsets sabotage your celebration. Give credit to yourself. Allow yourself to enjoy your accomplishments.

Don't let disappointments derail your progress. There is always sadness and grief when part of the plan doesn't work or it's hard to see around an obstacle. This is a good time to acknowledge that you are disappointed, but don't get stuck there. Don't cling to what doesn't work. Keep going.

Adjust your target. Don't let rigid expectations get in the way of your goals. We all learn along the way, and the process of change brings new information. Are you learning that you like to work out in the evenings rather than mornings? Did a new job, new family member, or new semester alter your workload? Examine what is working, as well as what isn't working as you make a change. Allow new circumstances to become part of your plan.

Enjoy the rewards. Look back over your journey of change, and recognize the benefits you are experiencing every day because of it. Intentionally doing this will help you maintain your changed behavior and patterns. Use this information to keep the change current in your life.

It is incredibly easy to drift into old habits and mindsets. Prevent that by incorporating the new feelings, abilities, and realizations you have found. The journey is never the destination. There will always be new changes to be made, and new visions and goals to grasp. Celebrate and keep the rewards you have worked so hard to achieve; this will keep you from having to repeat the process of change again and again. Then, you are ready for what's next.

Remember that change is opportunity. When we focus on one change at a time and slowly build that change into our life, we are living according to a long-term perspective, which over time will provide us with a better life. The ability to change our patterns of thinking, attitudes, and behaviors is critical to the development of our character and integrity. Recognizing what's not working in our lives and prioritizing what needs to change yields positive results and benefits.

The next chapter will emphasize the importance of goals. We'll look at how to make them and set them in a timely manner.

Chapter 2: Goal Setting

If you don't know where you are, how will you know where you are going? Goal setting is important, so let's start by defining what we mean when we talk about goals. Goals are future-oriented sets of criteria that are predetermined and achieved in a specific timeframe.

There are different types of goals, depending on how they are classified. For example, we can have goals in terms of timing, such as short-term, intermediate, and long-term goals. In the short term we can set goals for what we want to do in the next year. Intermediate goals might cover the next five years, while long-term goals may be set for ten years or more.

Aside from timing, another way we divide goals is by situation or setting, including:

- **Family:** Within the setting of family, there may be goals. What are our goals as a family unit this year or month? What are our goals in life as a family? You might like to consider your values as a family and question whether or not your goals embrace your family values.
- **Work:** These goals may be determined by ourselves, supervisors, or colleagues to complete a certain task or to change positions or roles in a company.

- **Organizations and associations:** We may have individual goals for our commitment and participation. However, the group may also set goals for the organization's level of success or outreach.
- **Professional:** Ask yoursef how to improve your professional standing or skills. Consider taking a class, renewing your certificate, or getting a license in something new, etc.
- **Personal:** Ask yourself, "What are my goals, personally, for this year? What do I want to do?" The topics of these goals may include improving one's health/diet, athletic development, hobby development, expansion of knowledge, membership in a club, etc.

The answers to these questions are the beginning of narrowing down and setting a goal. And you may find that some of these goals overlap in terms of situation. For example, a goal to improve your literacy skills in a computer program might advance you in your career/professional life.

Let's go back to the example of health and fitness. I've asked myself these questions: "Do I want to eat healthy this year? How much do I want to eat at one time, and how many times a day? If I want to exercise regularly, what kind of schedule should I set?" Answering these questions is a good way to start setting a personal goal for health and fitness.

Taking Stock

This leads us to my statement at the beginning of the chapter: "If you don't know where you are, how will you know where you are going?" Goal setting has to start with taking stock of where you are right now. If I want to weigh under 160 pounds by the end of the year, I have to get on the scale and find out what my weight is now. Or let's say I want to get my bachelor's degree within four years. I have to know how many credits I have now, as well as how many credits I will need to complete the degree. We must understand our current situation and work it into the process of setting goals.

S.M.A.R.T. Goals

This is a popular framework for goal setting. This was first developed by George Doran, James Cunningham, and Arthur Miller in 1981. It can be applied to organizations or individuals. The acronym stands for specific, measurable, attainable, relevant, and timely.

Specific means you want to set a goal that is not too general. In our health and fitness example, a specific goal is: "I want to go to the gym three times a week." This is better than: "I want to increase the number of times I go to the gym." Because if I'm not going at all right now, I could just go once this year and technically that would be an increase!

Measurable indicates that you have to figure out a way to see that you are improving. In our weight loss example, I have to be able to measure and track my weight. I might weigh myself every Monday for the next two months (*specific*) with the desire to reduce my weight by one pound a week *(measurable)*. I can't just think I'm losing weight by looking in the mirror; it must be more measurable than that.

Achievable reminds us that we should not set goals that are too high or cannot be realized. There may be a fine line here between our aspirations and achievable goals. This is a complicated area. While we want to be careful about setting goals that are unreasonable or unreachable, we also want to set goals that motivate us and give us something to drive toward. There is further discussion about how to gather information for goal setting in the previous chapter.

Relevant helps us choose a goal that is related to the overall goals. This point often comes up in companies and organizations. While it might be helpful to pursue some initiatives, they must be analyzed in terms of overall financial or production goals.

Realistic is another word that may be used in this acronym. For example, I want to expand my business because I believe it is valuable and beneficial. However, it is not practical to expand so quickly that staff are spread thin. So, it's more realistic to partner with other clinics or organizations where there is a supportive organizational structure and knowledge base. Thus, thinking choices through and meeting milestones on the way to achieving a long-term goal is often suggested in order to make transitions smoother.

Timely points out that the goal be set within reasonable time limitations. This also reflects on the relevancy of the goal. In some cases, goals must be achieved within a certain time frame, or they will no longer be needed. Deadlines and due dates need to be met in order for the overall goals to be reached. This is often the case when there are individual goals that make up an overall project or initiative.

What are the advantages of goal setting?

Setting goals can be very rewarding; it gives us a personal sense of purpose and satisfaction, especially when we are getting toward the end of the goal. Goals keep us accountable to ourselves and others. And they give us opportunities to make better decisions and change circumstances in our lives. Goals can help us prioritize and focus on what is most important.

What are the disadvantages of goal setting?

However, there could also be some disadvantages to setting goals. If we are not careful, goals that are too strict can lead to stress and risky behavior. For example, if you want to visit all fifty states before reaching a certain age, this could lead to overspending your travel budget or making plans to visit during dangerous weather or less than ideal circumstances. Another disadvantage to some goal setting is disappointment when goals aren't reached, and that can lead to increased stress. This scenario reinforces the idea that it's best to set goals that are achievable.

As we measure our progress toward goals, it's important to recognize progress and success in intermediate steps. Celebrating our achievements along the way increases the motivation to continue the journey. As we reach milestones, especially for long term goals, it is important to embrace the small achievements. This may look like going away for a long weekend with family and/or friends.

In the next chapter, we will learn about mindsets and how understanding these patterns can help you know yourself, as well as better negotiate your relationships with those around you.

Chapter 3: Understanding Your Mindset

Your mindset is powerful. How would you describe it? Is it that of a child, a teenager, or an adult? Or bits and pieces of all three? There are hidden pieces of our mindsets that affect how we think, manage our relationships, or even influence our perception of time. Understanding our own mindset is an important aspect of personal development. Additionally, becoming more aware of the mindsets of those around us can lead to better relationships and communication. As part of my life journey and training, I saw a professional psychologist, Dr. Kathleen Kelly of SYRONA Counseling Retreats, to better understand my own mindset, and that helped me a great deal.

Here is a brief summary of the three mindsets I mentioned above:

The Child

Mindset

A child's perception is innocent and naïve. The primary goal of childhood is to survive. Their needs must be met by others, and because of that, they are vulnerable. When under stress, we can all regress to this more primitive, or early, stage of development.

Thinking

Children believe what they are told, and childhood is a time of magical thinking, which we see reflected in today's theme parks and movies—filled with imaginary creatures, places, and stories. Being caught up in magical thinking doesn't leave much room for detailed, logical thinking. However, when this mindset begins experimenting with logical thought, it can take the form of narrow opposites—all or nothing, good or bad, black or white. There is a lack of complexity with no in-betweens. You are either alive or dead.

Feeling

Children show their feelings from the inside out. Unless the child has suffered trauma, their feelings are usually clearly visible. They are clearly happy, mad, or sad. In addition, feelings are believed to be caused by other people or external circumstances.

Relationships

A child is helpless in their relationships. They allow other people to define them and are unable to participate in an equal, independent relationships. The focus is on survival and safety, often needing approval or acceptance in order to feel okay about themselves.

Perception of Time

Time is never-ending in a child's mind. They won't understand why it is necessary to leave the amusement park when it closes for the day. When they are happy, it seems to them that they will always be happy. When they are upset, they might feel as though it will also last forever.

Now, examine your own feelings, behaviors, and attitudes in certain situations. Do you ever see yourself operating in a child's mindset?

The Teen

Mindset

A teen's perception is internally focused and selfish. This is our natural, or default, state. It is concerned about the teen, and no one else.

Thinking

Teenage thinking is simple and concrete; their ideas are set. There is a lack of experience, and the challenge of the teenage years is to develop the ability to think in more complex and abstract ways to incorporate the perspective of others. This is the process of developing an understanding that reaches beyond the individual's mental and sensory information. We can then apply these skills to become the adult mindset.

Feeling

There is a shallowness to the feelings experienced by teens. If it feels bad, it is wrong. If it feels good, it is right. In addition, the teenager is not able to manage their feelings well, so when frustrated, a teen can explode with absolute anger and tears. They are subject to impulsivity and urgency in both thoughts and actions.

Relationships

Teenage relationships have a push or pull aspect. The teen wants to be independent and pull away, but they still need parents and other authority figures, so they are conflicted between these two opposing forces. Another aspect of the teenage mindset is that it wants to win at all costs. Decisions to act are not made with the group in mind, but only in light of self-interest. Allowing for the perspective of others feels like losing.

Perception of Time

When it comes to time, the teen mindset is a tiger by the tail: they want what they want and they want it *now*. This impulse toward instant gratification reminds me of the Bible story about Esau and Jacob. Because Esau was hungry, Jacob was able to extract a high price for a bowl of stew. Esau handed over his rights as the oldest son in the family to his brother Jacob for the price of a single meal.

Now, examine your own feelings, behaviors, and attitudes in certain situations. When do you see yourself operating with a teenage mindset? How rigid are you? Can you view both the good and bad in a person at the same time?

The Adult

Mindset

The adult mindset maintains a complex point of view. It is able to go deep and examine subjects carefully. This mindset is where healthy relationships with ourselves and others are possible.

Thinking

Adult thinking is critical and broad-minded. There is an ability to be self-reflective and incorporate multiple perspectives. It uses logical reasoning.

Feeling

Facts are separated from feelings with adults. Those with an adult mindset are able to identify their feelings or emotions when considering a decision, experience, or incident. They are able to work through their feelings and are not defined or controlled by them. They are not afraid of feelings, and recognize them as one of the many sources of information.

Relationships

Relationships approached with the mindset of an adult are all-inclusive; it is about us—not just me.

Perception of Time

The adult mindset is able to time travel between the past and the future, as well as the present. It is informed by the past and considerate of the future, while being grounded in the present. The adult mindset can wander freely in the past without getting lost, or triggered, from past trauma. It also can calmly contemplate possible future circumstances.

Now, examine your own feelings, behaviors, and attitudes in certain situations. Do you see yourself operating in an adult mindset all the time? That is the goal. For example, when you are driving a car, are you in a teen mindset or an adult mindset? Different situations may trigger different mindsets and reactions, but don't let your emotions dictate your actions. Go with the adult mindset and keep emotions out of the driver's seat. They should be the passenger in the car.

In the next chapter, we will learn how these strategies can help us as we put the focus on our character. Developing our character can help us become better people marked by successful and productive lives.

Chapter 4: Developing Your Character

When I was young, my father employed about five men to cut the grass. I remember asking him, "Why don't you just get a lawnmower? You could have one person cut all the grass instead of five men!" He looked at me and said, "These five men have wives and children. By employing them, they're able to feed their families. If we got rid of four of them and bought a lawnmower instead, where would the other four get the finances to feed their families?" I never forgot that story, and I never will. It showed how my father honored his responsibilities to the community with unselfishness and compassion. He had an "adult mindset"—he was thinking of others, not just himself or his family. He chose to care for those around him.

What Is Character?

You are born with your personality. It lasts over time and does not change in different circumstances. However, you choose your values over time through experiences, choices, and relationships. And your personality and values help to create your character. *Your character is who you are and what you do when no one else is looking.* It is your character that emanates your reputation and personal integrity.

I suggest that character traits are built on universal ideas, which include humility and knowing and practicing a set of healthy values. These might include being fair, open, and transparent, practicing self-discipline, and having respect for other people, as well as compassion for their flaws. In the Bible, the apostle Paul highlights the fruits of the Spirit, which reflect good character: love for other people, joy and peace even when circumstances are not ideal, being patient with others, being kind and faithful and gentle, practicing self-control, and choosing to do the right thing.

Look over the list of values provided. Think about which are the most meaningful to you now. You may choose from this list or create your own values.

Personal Values	Social Values	Professional Values
• Achievement	• Independence	• Competence
• Commitment	• Loyalty	• Cooperation
• Knowledge	• Respect	• Work/Life Balance
• Family	• Safety	• Job Security
• Health	• Security	• Collaboration
• Generosity	• Vulnerability	• Recognition
• Love	• Justice	• Resourcefulness
• Relaxation	• Service	• Leadership
• Understanding	• Sense	• Efficiency
• Care	of Belonging	• Integrity
• Compassion	• Community	• Vision
• Gratitude	• Diversity	• Growth
• Generosity	• Equality	• Success
• Faith	• Culture	• Objectivity
• Excellence	• Contribution	• Opportunity
• Friendship	• Connection	• Reliability
• Honesty	• Morals	• Reason
• Forgiveness	• Environment	• Development
• Creativity	• Freedom	• Flexibility
• Courage	• Peace	• Wealth
• Patience	• Resiliency	• Expansion
• Fun		• Communication

Personal Values	Social Values	Professional Values
• Honor • Pride • Simplicity • Wisdom • Travel		

For example, as a Christian, my number one value is my relationship with God. Next is my relationship with my wife, and third, my relationship with my children. Those three things come before my relationship with anybody or anything else, including the workplace. A single person may not have the same set of values. They might rank their relationship with work before their relationship with their family. No matter what your values are, the first step is to identify them and put them in order. This will not only help you understand your character but will also help you make quick decisions when necessary (see Chapter 9: How to make Decisions). Whether the decision involves choosing between different jobs or choosing a new car, you can use the same principles.

Consider which of the values in the list are the most important to you during this phase of your life. Use the table below to prioritize your values.

Most Important Values	Somewhat Important Values	Less Important Values
1.	1.	1.
2.	2.	2.
3.	3.	3.
4.	4.	4.
5.	5.	5.

How Do You Develop Good Character?

Since your personality is not the same as your character, it doesn't always put up a strong defense against certain conditioned behaviors. Deeply ingrained, unacceptable tendencies may be especially difficult to uproot during the process of developing a good character. Good character builds over time, and you must have a humble personality for real character to grow well. Most people agree that a person of good character has positive values. These are expressed in the way you treat yourself, your colleagues, people with higher authority than yourself, and people with less authority than yourself as well.

Good character traits are very apparent in your work ethic. Ask yourself these questions to get some clarity about *your* character: Do you treat people with respect? Are you careful to not take advantage of vulnerable people? Do you act with humility (especially when working on something that is your strength)? Do you avoid taking your own revenge? Do you have the ability to bounce back when you fall down—to pick up the pieces and move on? All of these responses are indicators of your character.

Talent versus Character

Furthermore, a lot of people make the mistake of confusing talent with character. Talents are your God-given gifts and abilities. The way you use your talents reflect on your character, but your character is not determined by your gifts.

We are all familiar with famous people in high-profile industries, such as sports and music, who become rich. However, while they may make their first million based on their talents for athletics or songwriting, popularity that derives from a general perception of positive character traits often generates even more money for these individuals. Conversely, the fact that they can do something very well does not necessarily mean they are also of a good character. Your talent can only get you so far. It is your character that helps with the final leg of the journey to your destiny.

Developing Your Character

Your character evolves as a series of thoughts leading to behavior, which in turn develop into a pattern. These consistent thoughts and patterns of behavior reinforce your character. For example, if someone does not value timeliness and is consistently late to meetings, over time, everyone will get to know that they are latecomers. For better or worse, their lateness becomes part of their perceived identity or one of their character traits. Identity is an umbrella term that incorporates one's personality, their values, and their character.

It is easier to adopt good character if you have healthy role models to follow. It is much harder if you surround yourself with people of negative character or do not have good role models in your life. As the saying goes: "Show me who your friends are and I will show you who you are." Those you choose to spend your time with are significant. To develop good character, you need to surround yourself with people of similar or better values. You cannot excel or improve in character outside the five people closest to you. Who are your five? Who are the closest people in your life? These five have the greatest influence on you, so it's very important that they be of good character.

Another way to develop your character is to be proactive. A wise person sees danger ahead and avoids it. You must be intentional and pay attention. Go the extra mile for people and avoid shortcuts.

How does somebody develop the traits inherent in a strong character? It helps to be born into a family that has high moral values, religious beliefs, and strong work ethics, but not everybody is. If you have been raised in a family with limited character, you can still take ownership and create your own set of values. First, you need to learn how to manage your own emotional distress. Reaching out to a counselor would be a good way to begin. Be intentional in educating yourself and be an excellent worker if you are employed. You must be persistent and consistent. Always remember that *kindness is more important than wisdom.*

There is a real-life story that inspired a popular animated movie that illustrates this very well. In the 1200s, there was a prophecy given to King Naré Maghann Konaté (the king of West Africa's Mali Empire) that his son would be the greatest king that ever lived. This seemed impossible when his son, Sundiata was born crippled. But one day, out of sheer will and to rise above the hurtful remarks of others, Sundiata decided to walk, and this determination changed his life. The people started to recognize him as their true king and leader.

Then King Naré Maghann Konaté suddenly died before offering his son the throne and his mother became fearful for his life. She believed the king's other wife and son might kill her family and rule instead. She took Sundiata and her other children and left the palace in chaos. Soon King Soumaoro Kante of the Sosso attacked and took over the kingdom, and the people began to search for Sundiata to convince him to return and rule, which he did. Once he regained control of his father's empire he adopted for himself the title "Mansa," which means king or emperor. However, the people called him the Lion King, based on part of his name, "Sundi" that means "lion."

Had Sundiata listened to the voices around him, he would never have risen to greatness. His persistence to walk in spite of his deformity and then to return to power in the face of extreme conflict to aid his beloved kingdom shows that his love for the people was more of a priority than his personal safety. He knew who he was and acted on it.

The development of your character depends on knowing your true identity. This is not what society dictates, and may not be what your friends think, or even what your teachers and parents think. Character starts with knowing what you value and prioritizing it. But everyone must choose their own values to live by. It will vary from person to person.

Here are some fun questions to help you think about your character. As you answer them, they will help you see your values.

1. What is the name of your favorite superhero and why? Fill in the table and think through some of your favorite superheros' values.

Your Superhero	Their Values	Why do these values resonate with you?

2. What agitates or irritates you? What gives you that "I wanna choke that person!" feeling?

3. If you could do anything for free without getting paid, what would it be?

4. When you finally die, what do you want people to say or write about you? What do you want your legacy to be?

What If You Fail?

What if you've always failed? As I write this, I can recall several times that I have failed—as a son, father, and husband. If you don't make mistakes and learn from them, how can you be successful? It doesn't matter that you've had negative character traits during your lifetime; you can change. And guess what? You can learn from these negative experiences. Failure can bring growth. You learn from your mistakes. Sometimes you have to fail over and over to learn the right way.

Not getting knocked down is not a good story. Getting up is a good story. There are many inspiring stories of athletes such as boxers or fighters being defeated and then getting up repeatedly, over and over, after getting knocked down. Getting up opens the door to new possibilities for you. When you fail, you can go back and reflect on the reason you failed and the effect your failures had on you, your friends, and your family. This can help you avoid making the same mistake again because you will notice the warning signs. It may even allow you to guide others to steer clear of making similar mistakes, which can be very motivating.

Failing also gives you insight into other ways of thinking. You learn better coping skills and are able to handle stressful situations better. Without character flaws or the experience of failure, you only have one single way to succeed. And it's a fragile one, unable to withstand the force of daily life and the challenges that will come upon you as you interact with others. However, if you fail once, twice, or even three times, you look at things through a fresh lens. You have done this before, so you know what detours to avoid and see a way through it.

When you have to start from scratch, you will make errors but will also discover new perspectives while rebuilding yourself. In other words, having a character flaw can be a motivating factor for you to be a better person. This difficult, even painful, experience has the power to transform you and make you more likeable and even successful in the future.

Exercises for Developing Character and Fixing Flaws

The first step is to know what you value. This might take a lot of introspection and digging. Look at those around you who you look up to—they could be your role models. Find out more about their patterns of thinking and behavior. Find a way to incorporate their mannerisms into your life. Next, try to spend time with them. Surround yourself with those you wish to emulate. You may have to be a little aggressive to make them your associates or mentors. Make sure you are involved in their lives. I can't emphasize this enough: You can't rise above the five people with whom you associate most. They are the ones who influence your character.

Next, you will want to purify your character. Here you will need to identify your flaws. Lay down your sense of pride and make an honest list of anything you have been avoiding. What makes you angry? What do you complain about? What triggers anxiety or fear? As you look at this carefully, take the time to write down what you see. The physical act of writing will help you internalize and think through your flaws. Writing this out helps you to understand your experiences logically, reflect, and progress in a positive way. Then go to the next step.

Ask for feedback from three to five people who know you. They can be friends, family, or colleagues. They should not be someone who is indebted to you, but someone who can be completely honest. Ask people who can tell you the truth, without any fear of repercussion. Ask them to tell you the following:

- five things you are really bad at and don't do well
- five things you could improve
- five things you do well, in which you excel

The last question is not just to soothe your ego. People are more likely to be honest with you if they are able to say something positive, rather than only negative responses. If you ask five people to talk to you about ten things you can improve, or that you are bad at, you might get as many as fifty character flaws to address.

Additionally, try to engage in other activities; learn about other cultures and other ways of thinking that are different from what you have assumed is normal. This is not going to be a quick fix. This is going to be a journey, even a marathon. And remember to be content in your journey.

I also suggest you engage one of your role models to be an accountability partner. Everyone needs people who will hold them accountable. When you set goals regarding a pattern of behavior, your accountability partners will check on you either weekly or during some prescheduled time. Ask them to question if you've been prioritizing your values and/or have achieved your goals.

If these exercises are not enough and you have a really significant character flaw, consider getting professional help. While everyone has character flaws, there are certain basic principles that most people agree should be upheld. If your behavior includes consistent harmful patterns, such as lying, avoiding responsibility, and manipulating others, it should be addressed. When you aspire to, or currently work in, positions of responsibility, it's imperative that you practice honesty and become a positive influence on those around you.

If an accountability partner is not enough or is not working for you, continue your journey by hiring a life coach with excellent references or going into therapy with someone who also has good references. You wouldn't take your car to a mechanic without checking the reputation of the garage, right? You would not order goods online without reading the reviews. Whoever you decide to hire as your life coach or therapist should be thoroughly researched.

Lastly, you should have moments of personal reflection. Spiritual guidance may help you identify character flaws or areas that are holding you back, and show you what you need to work on and who you need to be. Remember our story about the real-life Lion King? He did not allow his physical condition to restrain him, but returned to the kingdom and fought to take his rightful position back as King.

Addressing your issues and flaws can lead to a positive reversal of fortune, open opportunities for friendship, career development, and generational blessings. Developing a strong character will encourage respect from others as you earn their trust and are given more responsibilities.

This introduction to mindsets and character development will help us internalize positive values and emulate a distinguished persona as we learn to communicate more effectively. The next several chapters will explore different aspects of important skills needed for good communication.

Chapter 5: Communication Skills

I f we understand each other, there's generally a reduced chance of disagreements.

Communication is a very important life skill. It affects the relationship with your spouse, parents, children, siblings, and others. It's extremely frustrating when people can't really hear and understand each other. A breakdown in communication leads to conflict and disagreements among siblings, couples, friends, coworkers, and even strangers.

There are several dimensions involved with communication: the communicator, the audience, the message, and the environment. Communication is the ability to deliver a clear and concise message that is not subject to misinterpretation in an environment conducive to understanding, and it leaves room for action to be taken. Over the next several chapters, we will discuss several aspects of good communication.

The skills in this chapter are specifically outlined for those who have or will have careers that are more entrepreneurial.

Audience

To communicate effectively, you need to know your audience, know your message, and develop a sense of timing. In addition, your communication style must adapt, depending on differences among groups of people. In fact, the audience can determine how messages are expressed. For example, if the audience belongs to a profession or church, that might also affect how you deliver your message. If you are communicating with individuals or small groups, engaging different communication skills may be appropriate.

You must become aware of cultural differences when you address others, and take this into account when you listen to them as well. There is also the need to be able to communicate with different age groups. You would not use the same style to communicate with pre-schoolers, high schoolers, young adults, or older age groups, because you don't want to miscommunicate and lose your audience. The good thing is that it can be addressed.

Here are some examples when considering your audience:

- Preschoolers: To get and keep young children's attention it's best to use many sensory objects, colors, characters, and different tones of voice.
- Teenagers: When talking to the youth today you would want to be direct and straight to the point as they are used to getting information quickly and concisely. You may lose their interest if you are longwinded.
- Older adults: Since older adults have patience, time, and wisdom, they would typically appreciate more thorough and thoughtful communication.

Knowing your audience is an important factor to take into consideration when building effective communication tactics. The message also needs to be appropriate.

Your Message

A good message should include the following five components:

- Clear vision and mission
- Resources to achieve that mission

- Adequate skills, knowledge, and ability on the part of those who will carry out the mission
- Incentives for those carrying the message out and consequences for those who do not adhere to its instructions
- Action plans for the content of the communication and ways to measure the results

Here's an example of these five steps being put into action. There is a remedy for treatment-resistant depression called Transcranial Magnetic Stimulation (TMS). If I had a desire to help treat people who suffer from depression, this would be my vision. Then, my mission would be to target the particular population of central New York and I would offer free consultations. I would have to evaluate the resources I have in order make this idea a reality. Since I only have one TMS machine, it would take me four days to treat one hundred people. But if I wanted to treat one hundred people in one day, I would need access to four machines. So I would either need to buy or borrow the TMS machines from somewhere. Once I had a hold of three more machines and established a location, I would need to hire and train technicians to properly implement all the components to begin the process. As far as incentives are concerned, I would need to appeal to highly qualified technicians with a good compensation. If necessary, the consequence of not being unable to fulfill their duties would be letting them go. However, getting the plan into action would require a social media blast to share the location and times we are available. Additionally, we would hold a meeting to prepare staff for the opening day. They would need to understand my expectations and their roles. Our secretaries would monitor the responses of interested people. By reviewing these numbers at the end of the day, we would compare them to those who made appointments versus those who wanted free consultations.

When you don't have a clear vision and mission in your message and don't take the time to clarify the content, confusion results.

Even if you have enough resources, and the people you're communicating with have the skills and behaviors to implement your plan, they will not be able to if they do not understand your message. If there are no resources to help execute what you want, such as time, money, or information, there will also be frustration because the people with whom you are communicating do not have what they need to complete the mission. Clear communication and adequate resources in the absence of skills, abilities, or knowledge just increases anxiety further because your audience is not equipped to undertake your plan.

When I was a medical intern, I was told to cover the cardiac unit, but I did not know what to do if someone went into cardiac arrest! When working that shift, I was riddled with anxiety. I just could not function. Thankfully no one went into cardiac arrest, because I would not have known how to help them! So, in this situation, I had a clear mission and resources but not the knowledge or skills to truly help if someone was in need.

Lastly, if all the other components exist, but you do not have an action plan or any guidelines, people will do what they want, and your mission will not produce the desired fruit.

Planning for clear communication should take tone, tact, strategy, trust, truth, and teamwork into consideration. If this were to take place in a meeting, it would be crucial for the host to set a positive, respectful, and professional tone with the attendees. Additionally, most meetings would have an agenda to keep everyone focused and engaged. Next, in order for there to be trust and truth, the host would have to create a safe space for attendees to feel comfortable enough to share their honest opinions. If the meeting meets these criteria, roles can be established for next steps and teamwork will flow easily.

Ultimately, there should be a synchrony between the ones giving and receiving the message. If these are lacking, the message may not get through or may be easily forgotten. When we learn how to communicate effectively, everyone feels heard. Better planning has the potential to greatly increase your chances of getting your message across and having influence over its outcomes.

In summary, effective communication that is designed to achieve a plan should have clear vision and mission with adequate resources for what you want others to do. The audience should have the appropriate skills, abilities, and knowledge to carry it out. There should be an action plan and the consequences of not carrying out the instructions should be clear as well. When these five components are achieved together, you are more likely to be successful. But what happens when there is a conflict—or if communication leads to conflict?

Conflict in Communication

When communication is out of sync, there is a greater risk of being misunderstood, misrepresented, misinterpreted, and frustrated. This leads to conflict and reduces any progress toward what you want to achieve. When there is conflict around our communication, we may be offended or react in three primary ways:

- **Shutting down**: This type of reaction suppresses our emotions and anger to the subconscious level. It may manifest in somatic symptoms, such as muscle aches and stomach aches, and may eventually lead to explosions of anger or lashing out. Usually, the explosive reaction is blown out of proportion when compared to the issue at hand. This happens because emotions have been suppressed. A buried feeling never dies.
- **No filter**: This is a reaction to a lack of understanding. It's a defense mechanism that is governed by the statement, "I will hurt you before you hurt me." They lash out and say hurtful things before anyone gets the chance to strike them first. This is why I strongly discourage people from responding or mak-

ing decisions when they are angry. Having no filter causes un-necessary damage to relationships with other people.

- **Gossiping**: Some people respond to a breakdown in commu-nication by gossiping. They share their perception of the con-flict with other people. This is a way to both respond to the offense and seek validation. Although this can provide some initial comfort, it is transitory and does not address the issue or take any steps toward conflict resolution. It may also make things worse.

To avoid these three reactions when you need to repair a break-down in communication, it's important to strive for the right timing, environment, and tone. That way, the person (or people) with whom you are communicating are able to hear and understand your message.

Another way to communicate when conflict arises involves prac-ticing restoration. This is ideal. When speaking with the offender, gather more information to understand their point of view. This will help you see how they came to certain conclusions. Have an open mind about their interpretations and perspective. Listening and "mir-roring" what the person says will help them feel heard and under-stood. Mirroring is repeating the last few words a person has said, once they finish speaking. The benefit is that they will feel comfort-able enough to continue the conversation and will be open to resolu-tion at the end. Restoration takes time and energy, and it is a sign of maturity to take the first step to reengage communication.

It's often helpful to apologize, even when you think the other person is wrong. It is important to take some responsibility. For example, if somebody tells me that my driving is rough, I have to accept that statement to some extent. An ideal response from me would be, "Thank you for telling me that. It would help to hear some specific examples." It's usually best to use "I" statements, or "I feel" statements, because this indicates less defensiveness on your part. Here's an example: "When you did not clean the bathroom, I felt taken advantage of." This statement is less likely to lead to conflict than, "You never clean the bathroom."

Life will have conflict. If you live and work with someone long enough, there will be conflict. View this as an opportunity for growth, not a means to master the art of arguing. You can use these conflict opportunities to learn, develop, and inspire others. Learning how to communicate effectively does much more than foster intimacy in relationships; it also has the potential to make you more influential when you get your message across.

Other Elements of Good Communication

Body language: The content of our speech accounts for only about twenty percent of how we communicate. We also communicate non-verbally through body language, posture, and eye contact. Body language is very important. If someone is fidgeting or shifting, it suggests increased anxiety or nervousness. When speaking or otherwise communicating, posture is important. By sitting down, leaning forward, and maintaining eye contact, we show that we are responding and contributing to the discussion. Ideally, both communicators should appear interested, ask follow-up questions, nod their heads, and respond with phrases such as, "Uh-huh." Small verbal responses along with overall body language go a long way to enhance effective communication.

However, it is important to understand the implications of non-verbal communication in the context of culture too. For example, people from some cultures may believe that prolonged eye contact is rude. However, in western culture, lack of eye contact may suggest that the person is not confident or not engaged in the conversation. The same can be said for posture. In some cultures, a slight inclination of the head during conversation is a sign of respect and active listening. It will be important to know and research your audience ahead of time.

The act of communication is a skill that needs to be learned, practiced, and perfected. Even the best communicator may experience periods when they are not able to deliver the message accurately. No matter how good you are at communicating, there may be a breakdown in communication that leads to conflict. The next chapter will address how to anticipate and resolve conflicts in communication—and how to recognize when (and if) it's better to let go.

Chapter 6: Conflict Resolution: Confrontation and Correction

Most people find it difficult to confront others. This is not surprising. Depending on how you were raised and the makeup of the people who surround you, you may be either non-confrontational or very confrontational. If you were raised in a family where everybody yelled at each other but nobody took the time to listen, you may have internalized this behavior and become confrontational. On the other hand, if your family didn't allow you to express a difference of opinion, you may be the reverse. Neither of these extreme positions lead to conflict resolution. So what's easier? To turn the other cheek and let it go? Or to bring up disagreements with other people?

Issues arise when you shy away from confrontation. A so-called "elephant in the room" situation leads to suppressed frustration and unconscious anger, which may manifest in somatic symptoms, such as lower back pain, high blood pressure, neck pain, fibromyalgia, and cardiovascular illnesses.

As Dr. John E. Sarno wrote in his book, *Healing Back Pain: The Mind-Body Connection*, having unconscious anger, being the nice guy and repressing anger in the face of current stressors exposes one to recurrent back pain.[1] In this case, the best treatment is to deal with the subconscious issues.

After finishing my residency at SUNY Upstate Medical University in Syracuse, New York, I was immediately appointed as an attending physician in the unit where I had just been a resident physician. I found myself working with senior colleagues and mentors. It was difficult for me to say no, and it was difficult for me to confront them when I thought they were wrong. To make matters worse, the nurses still referred to me as a resident!

I started developing low back pain, which I chronicled and tracked over time. In psychiatric services, we work with both matter and the mind. My subconscious rage had to come out, and when my colleagues and I were together it came out as low back pain. What is the standard treatment of low back pain? You go to a chiropractor, or to your doctor or a physical therapist, and if nothing works, they stick this huge needle in your back and give you a cortisone shot. I went through all of these treatments and nothing worked, until my then chairman, Dr. Dewan, gave me the book by Dr. Sarno.

I used his book to successfully treat myself, and that experience taught me that I could not ignore my unconscious rage and continue to avoid confrontation. *Not speaking your mind and turning the other cheek all the time doesn't work.* Even so, please don't think I'm suggesting confrontation is always the best answer or even necessary. Instead, it's important to create clear boundaries to prioritize your needs.

For example, there was a time early in my career when I would say yes to everything. I was trying to please and impress everyone. And in addition, I was approached to coach three of my children's soccer teams as well. This was a humbling request; however, my plate was already full. I had to say no to prioritize the needs of my family.

---

1. John E. Sarno, *Healing Back Pain: The Mind-Body Connection* (New York: Grand Central Publishing, 2019).

To Confront or Not Confront

The following steps are helpful in deciding whether or not to confront someone.

Get the facts! First, be sure you have the correct facts. You don't want to confront someone based on hearsay. Once you get all the facts, clarify the issue. Next, write down what you want to say. This helps a lot. When you write something down, you think about it more clearly. Look at the language and wording you are using. Read it aloud to yourself. You may want to run it by some trusted colleagues to see their reactions. Then approach the person with a neutral attitude. Don't confront someone when they are hungry, angry, tired, or after receiving bad news. Also, don't confront someone when you are having a bad day. You may want to let them know that you would like to talk to them at least twenty-four hours in advance, so they are ready to talk. If it is a sensitive matter, you may want to have another person with you. In addition, choose an appropriate setting and timing. It's important that you both feel comfortable in the setting.

Begin with a clear statement, such as, "I want to talk about X." It is quite possible that the person you want to confront may decide to admit their mistake, open up to you, and apologize. It may end right there. However, most of the time it doesn't end there, so move on to the next step. When you begin the confrontation, actually read from your notes. That way, if the person reacts angrily, or with irritation, you are less likely to be led by your own anger. You can stick to the script. Once you go through the facts and write down what you want to say, you are ready to present the issue and confront the person.

During the Confrontation

Here are some steps to use during the confrontation.

Make the meeting face to face. This will encourage empathy and allow you to share what's in your heart. This will also allow you to read their body language and facial expression, which may guide the depth of your conversation. Do not use email or text messages to the person with whom you want to communicate. During the meeting, look into the person's eyes and speak sincerely, showing confidence by sitting down and leaning forward. Most importantly, pick your battles! You don't have to confront everything; certain things need to be let go. This may seem like overkill, but I also recommend practice. Rehearse what you would like to say. You may want to record it and hear it yourself. Practice in front of the mirror, monitoring your eye contact, your facial expressions, your mouth and lips, and your shoulder position. As previously suggested, you may also want to practice with some of your colleagues or friends whom you know and trust. Ask for feedback. When you're practicing, try making yourself look empathetic or decisive. Now that you have it all together, you should go and confront the person.

During the meeting, start with positive affirmations and acknowledgement of the person you're confronting. Let's say you're confronting a coworker—you may want to start with statements such as, "You are a valuable person in this company. Your contributions include A, B, C, and D. However, there are some things we need to talk about." *Do not make up the positive affirmations*. Talk about their real accomplishments and attributes. If they are fake, it will not have the same power, as the person listening will probably catch on to the empty compliments. This may cause the person you are confronting to start from a calmer ground zero and quickly become hypervigilant or anxious. Once you make your initial statement about your concern, give them a chance to respond because you may get a response from them regarding the issue. That may be the end of the conversation.

After the initial reaffirmation of your regard for them, focus on the issue, not the person. For example, if the issue is that they are always late to work, let them know how that affects their colleagues and business functions. Do not use "you" statements like, "You are always late," or "You never do this." *Always* and *never* type statements describe extremes and exaggerate somewhat true statements. They do nothing to resolve the issue. That tactic will only make the person you are trying to gently confront angry. If the issue has to do with communication, use statements such as, "When you said that, I felt this." An example would be, "When you said I never dress well, I felt as though you didn't acknowledge all the thought I'm putting into this relationship." Use "I" wording because it shows you're ready to accept some responsibility. It can lessen the defensiveness of the person who is being confronted, and it shows your own sense of ownership and responsibility in the situation.

If the person you're confronting is resistant, angry, obnoxious, or loud, do not push it. Gently call off the meeting.

As I mentioned previously, you do not need to confront every issue. It's best to know when to let something go and when to confront issues that truly need to be addressed. This distinction depends on your core values. When possible, avoid confrontation, especially when it has the potential for negative consequences. It can lead to anger buildup and break down relationships and communication. People have lost jobs and friendships by not communicating effectively or, on the other hand, communicating aggressively or over-communicating. Either extreme is not productive.

There are benefits of confrontation other than resolving the issue according to your own plans. The discussion may expose your own blind spots. You can come away from the confrontation with a better understanding of the situation, more aware of your own biases or mis-interpretations. There are many ways that confrontation may change relational dynamics for the better. There may be health advantages like lowering blood pressure, tension, and anxiety. Or you may learn a few things about their perspective and how they understood the situation. Inevitably, the experience you gain through understanding how to con-front others with a positive outcome will strengthen your harmonizing skills and help you to also say no to sticky situations.

Why Do We Avoid Confrontation?

We avoid confrontations for several reasons. The first one is denial. Just because you don't want to acknowledge the problem, it doesn't make it go away. It is buried until surfacing in the future. Another reason we avoid confrontation is fear of disappointing others. If you have been raised to be a people-pleaser you may worry, "If I confront this person, what are they going to think of me?" The truth is that some people already think negatively of you with or without a confrontation. You could be Santa Claus and people might still hate you and still find a reason not to like you; therefore, having meetings to address issues, if done correctly, might weaken the tension.

This leads me to identify three categories of people in this mix.

Peace fakers are those who sweep things under the rug. They don't want to talk about the elephant in the room. They try to put off the disruption any way they can, but it will eventually come. When disruption finally erupts, they may not know how to handle it and ruin valuable or important relationships.

Peace breakers are wired to cause chaos, so in constant chaos, they justify their own role. They initiate conflict even when there is no need. They have sadistic pleasure when they rile other people up. It excites them.

Peacemakers are the last category. They follow the principles outlined in this chapter with the goal of fixing the problem, not to condemn someone or judge them.

Disclaimer: I'm not writing this as an expert. I have had several occasions when there was no peace. I have been both the faker and, more or less, the peace breaker, but I'm learning to be a peacemaker.

In the next chapter, we will explore how to say no. This is an important aspect of good communication and essential to our personal development.

Chapter 7: How to Say No

People do not want to say no for many reasons that may include:

- A desire to be well-liked
- A desire to please others
- Not wanting to disappoint others
- Wanting to avoid conflict
- In an effort to be unique (thinking they can accomplish the task, even if they cannot)
- Feeling of discomfort
- Fear of rejection
- To prevent being kicked out of the group/clan

Most people find it difficult to say no. Saying no is viewed as a negative attitude in certain contexts, but there are ways to say no effectively. If you are asked to do something, do not immediately give an answer either way. Respond by saying, "I will think about it." Then give yourself time to actually think about it.

After you have thought for a while, if your decision is no, share why you can't do it. Use phrases like, "I would like to do this, but I have already committed to (fill in the blank), therefore I don't have enough time to do (what you asked)." If adding a reason opens you up to further trouble, just say, "No, I can't."

Win with No

Saying no increases our credibility and helps our self-esteem. When it is appropriate, saying no can be helpful to you, your family, your health, and even the person to whom you are saying no. For example, if your boss gives you an opportunity to work overtime on a Sunday, but this is the day that you want to rest, you can respond by saying, "I would love to work, but I haven't spent enough time with my children this week and I need to take them to their soccer game." This is an example of saying no without sounding negative or worse—not saying no upfront.

A few years ago, I took a new job at a hospital where I had been working. I was aware of the job description of the person who held the position previously, but I was asked to take on more responsibilities, which were equivalent to two other jobs. I took the position, but requested that I get three months to settle into the original job description—without the added duties. I told my managers that this would help me acclimate to the new position. But in my mind, I wondered why they expected me to do the job of three people when the previous person had performed only one of those jobs! During the initial three months, I collected data on the workload I was completing compared to that of my new colleagues. I quickly realized I was doing more than double the work of others in the same amount of time.

After the three months concluded, I met with my managers and showed them the data. Needless to say, they were dumbfounded. As a result, I was able to avoid taking on the extra work. If I had initially said yes, I would have been drowning in work, not meeting the expectations of my managers, and needing three extra blood pressure medications. Although I took the job, I did not commit to what they were asking of me. I took the time to do my research and make sure that I would be equipped for the position. When I went back to my managers, I was able to subtly say no to the extra job responsibilities and save myself from extra stress.

Both these examples show how saying no can also help those who are making the request of you. If you need to take your children to a soccer game but you accept the overtime, then you will be distracted at work, perhaps resentful of your workplace, and conflict may be building at home. You may start looking for a new position because you are feeling too pressured, and your workplace will lose an experienced employee. If I had started in the new position at the hospital with a triple workload, the quality of my work would likely have suffered, the morale of my team might have been lowered due to my lack of attention and energy, and the institution would not have been dividing the workload properly. Planners would not have had the correct information for developing staffing plans or restructuring.

Please remember that the ability to say no can be developed. The back pain I experienced previously was because I lacked the ability to say no, but that experience helped me learn how to do it. You can learn this as well.

Practice Yes and No

When deciding how to answer demanding requests, you should seek counsel from people you trust before you agree to something. Others can help you assess the consequences of your answer and help you decide which will be a better option. Just make sure you decide what is best for you.

Saying no takes practice. Most people don't like to say no because they want to be well-liked; however, there is only so much responsibility a person can handle. Responding to a request by saying no when it actually matters can increase your credibility, productivity, and emotional wellness. It gives you time to focus on things that really matter to you. It also opens things up. Now they will find someone else for that project, so it opens up opportunity for others.

On the other hand, people may also say no to you. And they may say no when you expect them to say yes. Those you have helped, mentored, or sacrificed for may say no to you when you least expect it. This may lead to surprise, anger, and resentment in you. Since it is unhealthy to harbor these feelings, you need to be able to forgive. Forgiveness is discussed in the next chapter.

Chapter 8: Forgiveness

Not forgiving and choosing to remain angry is like drinking poison and hoping the other person will die. You may have seen some version of this popular sentiment.

What is forgiveness? Forgiveness involves an intentional and conscious process in which somebody who has been betrayed, violated, or wronged in any way is able to voluntarily let go of anger, resentment, rage, and hatred. Forgiveness is an act that is both conscious and selfish. It is done in order to free the one who is harboring resentment from bondage.

Breaking the bondage of anger and the other emotions associated with injustice takes an intentional decision. Forgiveness involves treating the person who offended you with compassion instead of vengeance. However, forgiveness does not mean a return to the previous relationship. It does not allow others to take further advantage. It does not condone or excuse the offender's behavior. It is not wishing for revenge or taking punitive action toward the offender, and it is certainly not having someone else take revenge on your behalf.

When we don't forgive, we are choosing to adopt a child mindset: everything is all good or all bad. It is like driving in the rain without working windshield wipers. Your ability to see clearly is obscured.

Have you harbored anger and unwillingness to forgive? How is that working for you?

Suffering the Consequences

Choosing the path of unforgiveness will have spiritual, psychological, and physical consequences. Spiritually, the inability to forgive, or holding on to offense, is one of the greatest obstacles to growth. It is like putting a block in front of you or dragging someone behind you. We must forgive those who have sinned against us. Our Creator commands us to forgive. According to the Bible, if we choose to not forgive, *then we may not be forgiven* by God.

> So if you are offering your gift at the altar and there remember that your brother has something against you, leave your gift there before the altar and go. First be reconciled to your brother, and then come and offer your gift. Come to terms quickly with your accuser while you are going with him to court, lest your accuser hand you over to the judge, and the judge to the guard, and you be put in prison (Matthew 5:23-25, ESV).

In other words, if we remember that our brother or sister has done something against us, we must go and make peace with our "sibling" before coming back to make our prayers and offerings. This suggests that our prayers are unlikely to be answered if we do not first forgive others. There is a delicate balance here, because forgiveness doesn't necessarily repair relationships, and reconciliation doesn't always result in restoration. But forgiveness does free the person who has been holding on to offense. Choosing not to forgive puts us in a prison of sorts, handicapping us spiritually and emotionally.

Lastly, I believe an inability to forgive is not compatible with love. You cannot claim to love someone unconditionally and still not forgive them. Loving someone fully means finding a way to forgive their transgressions.

There are also physical consequences when we don't forgive. Our heart depends on it, literally. Lack of forgiveness has been associated with a higher risk of heart attack, higher cholesterol levels, and physical pain as well as a lack of sleep. In addition, there has been evidence of high blood pressure! Conversely, being ready to forgive comes with huge rewards, including reduced risk of heart attack, lower cholesterol levels, better sleep, lower blood pressure, and less pain.

As for psychological consequences, resistance to forgiveness has been associated with increased anxiety, depression, and stress. Studies have shown that people who are naturally able to forgive and let go tend to have less anger, depression, and hostility. However, people who hold grudges often have severe depression and post-traumatic stress disorder in addition to other health conditions.

With all these consequences, you may be wondering why anyone would *not* choose to forgive. Holding on to past pain can be a coping mechanism. Drawing from anger and resentment releases cortisol and its accompanying adrenaline rush. Unfortunately, this extra cortisol in the body is damaging to the body and could have lasting effects.

Steps to Forgiveness

It's vital to understand that forgiveness does not mean forgetting. It is a conscious decision; you are admitting that you have been wronged and have decided to forgive. I recommend that people write down the event that was traumatic, including their reactions and feelings. Describe how the anger made them feel. Put your sense of shame on paper. What kind of pain did you experience in this situation? Lay it out. Now seek to have empathy for the person who has offended you, remembering that many people damage others because they have been damaged themselves.

The aforementioned system can be summarized into four phases:

1. Uncover the offense: Describe what has been endured, what happened, the reaction, and the feelings. Write down painful emotions, such as anger and shame. Note any behavior changes, such as avoiding relationships. Include psychological harm, such as recurring thoughts and nightmares. Go ahead and label these emotions and thoughts.

2. Decide to forgive: Intentionally write down what forgiveness means and what it would take for release. I suggest writing down the advantages *and the disadvantages* of deciding to forgive.

3. Release the feelings held toward the offender: This is where we have a lot of work to do. Release the uncomfortable feelings and replace your negative thoughts with positive ones. We often think before we are even aware of the feelings. Changing our negative thoughts and replacing them with positive thoughts can add momentum to the process.

4. Continue the forgiveness process: There are benefits that result from the initial forgiveness. By describing the injustice, the resulting personal growth may be more clearly witnessed. However, I must emphasize that forgiveness is not forgetting, but a self-healing process given to us by God. It aims to free us so that we don't remain in bondage. Once we live a life free of this baggage, we can sleep more soundly, avoid nightmares, and live as free people. It's not something that's easy to do. That's why it takes a conscious effort and work.

This list that you have completed represents the price tag behind that offense. It allows you to actually "count the cost" (another biblical principle found in Luke 14:28, which comes into play here). When you reckon the effect of an offense clearly on paper, you gain a perspective you will not appreciate by simply forgiving verbally. You force yourself to explore that offense right there in front of you in black and white: you did one thing, they did another, and it played out in this fashion. Each action connects to its corresponding hurt, and now that you have broken it into its pieces, you can seek help to develop empathy for the offender and be healed of the damage it did to you. Prayer and meditation and just spending time on it are all great helps in this process.

I want to share a personal story about someone I thought I had forgiven. I was working at a hospital and this coworker constantly annoyed and irritated me. She would do very minute and subtle things just to get under my skin. This continued relentlessly over a period of seven months with no end in sight. I decided that I wanted to forgive her, and made a conscious decision to do so. I wrote everything down, stating that I wanted to completely forgive her.

However, a few months later, a horrible rage came over me when I saw her walking down the hallway. I felt that if I could get a hold of her, I would choke her! I clearly had more work to do in my forgiveness of her actions. Forgiveness is not necessarily a one-stop, one-action process; very often, it is a continuous and constant action that may last a long time. We need to make a decision to forgive once, twice, and sometimes even more.

The good news is that there are limitless advantages to the power of forgiveness. It is truly a win-win. Forgiveness frees you up to move and breaks the chain (or anchor) that holds you down, allowing you to make wise and informed decisions.

Chapter 9: How to Make Decisions

Most individuals find it difficult to make decisions. Sometimes the process is confusing, especially when we are confronted with two different choices:

- "Should I take extra work?"
- "Should I go to my daughter's soccer game?"

It's hard to know which choice is better, but there is a method that might make your decision-making process simpler.

Establish Your Priorities

Values are actions manifested by your priorities. So, before establishing your priorities, review the list of values you created earlier in this book. Be sure that your priorities fall in line with your values and not the other way around. From there, it will be easier to list your priorities in order of importance. For example, if your family is the most valuable to you, you would prioritize your child's school play over staying late at work. If you value your religion over your favorite sports team, you would be in church on Sunday instead of skipping it to watch your favorite team play.

Using the given table, copy the same list you created in Chapter 4: Developing Your Character. Then rank your current priorities from most important to least important. On your first attempt, your values and priorities may not align horizontally. Look at the table again. How can you rearrange your priorities to better match up with your values? Generally speaking, your values are fixed, and your priorities are flexible.

My Values	My Priorities
1.	1.
2.	2.
3.	3.
4.	4.
5.	5.

Now you have a tool to help make your decisions based on the hierarchy of your own values. (This will also help you protect yourself from investing in things outside those values.) However, priorities change over time, so remember to revisit and reevaluate your list.

When you need to make decisions regarding two or three areas of conflicting interests, you can revisit this list and review how you ranked your values. This may not work for everybody or in every case, but it offers additional assistance in helping you make decisions quickly. The process may still be difficult at times, but could be less so in many areas.

One thing is certain in life: we will continue to make decisions. In elementary school, we must decide what we want for lunch; in high school, which classes to take; in college, what major to choose. Most importantly, we choose our life partner. Procrastination over decisions can drag on for days, weeks, months, or even years. Many people don't realize that *not* making a decision *is a decision*. Being unintentional and just going along with a situation does not mean a good decision was made. It is therefore necessary to have the skills, abilities, and experience to be able to make timely and well-thought-out choices.

Let's make this simple. There are so many books out there about how to make decisions. However, I am recommending that you make your decisions based on your own set of values. The most difficult part of this process is the one you began with here: listing and ranking your values and matching them to your priorities. You must take the time to think this through.

When making a decision, you can pull out this list. Use it to help you make big decisions by arranging the pros and cons of each choice: like choosing a job or buying a car. Then you can make your decision by choosing the one with more pros than cons. The same process can be applied when you want to buy a house. You may have a list of qualities that you want in your ideal house. Other than building your house from scratch, you will have to visit different houses to decide, based on your values, which house has more of what you need and want. This step requires a lot of time. It is important that you take the weeks (or months) necessary to list your priorities and values so you can see what is best. If you do this, it will become easier to make decisions going forward.

Evaluate the Impact of the Decision You're Making

Some decisions have lifelong, or even generational, consequences. For example, the choice of your spouse is not a decision that should be made lightly, as it will influence the direction of your entire life. Your choice in higher education may affect the type of relationships you are going to develop. Your career may be the deciding factor between future personal fulfilment and frustration in your job. It is important to be clear about each decision's objective, taking into account how it may affect your values, priorities, and future outcomes.

Explore Other Options

As mentioned above, it is best to consider the pros and cons before making a decision. It's also worthwhile to look at the alternative options. For example, you may want to buy a Mercedes Benz as a luxury car; however, you might find all the features you want in a Lexus or Audi, so looking around is a good idea. Once you have all the information, you can go back to your guiding set of values. In the case of a car, maybe you want one with advanced safety features or a car that's very comfortable. Maybe you want a car with all-wheel drive rather than front-wheel drive. When you fall back on your values, it will help you to make a decision regarding what to buy and what not to buy.

Talk It Through with Trusted People

Once you have made a decision, talk it over. Look for well-informed people with experience in the area you are exploring. Talk about how it turned out. Look for people who are not biased. In the case of a car, talk to people who have bought the model of car you are considering, and ask about their experience after purchase.

Test Your Decision-Making Ability

Practice making decisions. You are going to make mistakes, but use them as opportunities for growth. You can learn from the past. Do not groan and moan about every poor decision you have made; just make sure you do not repeat the same mistake twice!

Take Action

Once you have written your set of values, measured the pros and cons, sought advice from others, specifically spoken with those who have made similar decisions in the past, it's time to be decisive and take action.

Let me share a personal example with you. When I went to visit my son in college, it was supposed to be a three-day trip. However, on the third day my son became ill and was taken to the hospital. As a physician, I had patients booked for the following week. On Sunday, when we were supposed to return home, I was torn between staying with my son and going back to work.

However, because I had my values plainly set, it was easy. My son came before my job. I did not even have to think about it very long. I decided to stay with my son. Some people may say, "You could have been fired!" That is true. But in my mind, not spending that time with my son had more negative consequences than the loss of my job. Being a father has a greater priority than my job. Sometimes we forget to actually spend time with our children and be present with them. Recreational activities are important but cannot replace personal, quality time. That time is what our children will remember when they grow older and leave home. Trust me, time flies by. This was an easy decision for me, but not all decisions will be that simple.

Another example of a rather complicated decision was whether to travel during COVID-19. A friend of mine lost his father in a far-away country during the pandemic. In the tradition of his country, you were supposed to go and be involved with the funeral of your own father. However, there were significant restrictions during the pandemic. He had to make a choice between taking the risk of catching COVID-19 during the trip or letting down his relatives by not appearing at the funeral. I did not envy my friend's choice. In the end, he made the decision to stay home and have the funeral proceed without him. He has to live with the repercussions of that decision for the rest of his life. However, he realized that if he had gone overseas, he may have subjected himself and his family to COVID-19, in addition, he may have been quarantined in a foreign country with no guarantee of coming back to the United States.

Some decisions are relatively easy to make, like the first example about my son, and others are more difficult. One way or another, you will make decisions. Even if you think you are not making them, you are. Be aware that sometimes, by not actively making a decision and perhaps going along with the expectations of others or by just following society's rules of behavior, you are still passively making a decision. This may have unforeseen consequences. When you lack decisiveness, it may lead to further procrastination. This common behavior is a great waste of time, but correctable. We will address this in the next chapter.

Chapter 10: Procrastination

A procrastinator is one with a regular habit of putting things off until later, either through fear, laziness, or indecisiveness. Unfortunately, a continuous pattern of procrastination leads to serious character flaws. However, almost everyone procrastinates in one way or another. Studies have shown that fifty percent of people have not drawn up a will or have one that is out of date or incomplete when they die. The potential consequence for not doing it is that fifty percent of your assets can be taken by the government. In addition, you may leave your loved ones in a state of chaos and unnecessary struggle immediately after your demise.

There is also significant evidence showing that putting off important tasks leads to cardiovascular stress. This additional stress increases cortisol levels and makes us more susceptible to illness. Prolonged procrastination has also been linked to headaches, gastrointestinal problems, and lack of sleep.

A psychologist named Fuschia M. Sirois has suggested that people who are procrastinators are likely to put off important health behaviors, such as starting regular exercise, stopping smoking, or going to the doctor. These are clearly harmful strategies. In one study, Sirois included a sample of 182 people who had a diagnosis of high blood pressure or cardiovascular disease. She measured this group against a sample of

584 healthy people. The entire test group took an online survey to measure their level of procrastination. Survey results showed that the group with hypertension and cardiovascular disease scored a lot higher on their level of procrastination compared with the healthy control group. Additionally, the subgroup with high blood pressure and cardiovascular disease showed a much stronger association with maladaptive coping strategies, such as behavioral disengagement, a lack of self-compassion, and a tendency toward self-blame.

Along with behaviors that don't support personal health, there are other consequences associated with procrastination.

Wasting Precious Time

One of the worst things about procrastination is that when you let that time go, you cannot get it back. Our time is precious and, once gone, cannot be lived again. Nevertheless, when you don't get something done, it robs you in substantial ways. When a task is not being taken care of, recurring thoughts about it can circulate and sometimes torment the mind, including regret and frustration. The eventual performance of the task, perhaps in less ideal circumstances, does not usually produce the best work you could have done. As a result, there may be a reduction in personal satisfaction and a sense of inherent shame associated with the halfhearted job. In the end, the consequences of inaction may also be time consuming,

If you continually procrastinate, it will be difficult, or almost impossible, to meet your goals. Setting goals is just the beginning; you also have to do the work.

Procrastination causes you to miss precious opportunities. Opportunities don't always come, and if you don't seize them, you may not get a second chance at them. It is possible to waste and miss them simply because you are not prepared for or intimidated by them.

The person who continually procrastinates may develop poor self-esteem. Achievements build confidence and so does learning from mistakes. Both are necessary for a healthy self-image. You cannot achieve success or develop strategies for future success if you do not first attempt the task or don't think you can do it.

Procrastination damages your reputation. When you give your word and say you're going to do something and then don't do it, people lose trust in you. A continual pattern of this leads to a tarnished reputation. So procrastination hurts your reputation *and* your self-esteem. People will stop depending on you and quit taking your word seriously.

If you procrastinate, you may be forced to make decisions in a hurry, and when you don't have the time to think through the decision-making process, you may make the wrong decision.

It also affects your work performance. If your boss gives you tasks to complete, but you continue to procrastinate and are not able to make deadlines and don't hit the targets, you will get fired from your job. Similarly, if your teacher assigns a project and it is not done in a timely manner, it will affect your grades and more.

As mentioned above, there are studies linking procrastination to cardiovascular diseases. However, health effects are not limited to physical problems. Psychological problems, such as bouts of depression or anxiety, may also result from continuous procrastination. If you promise you are going to do something for someone and you don't do it, procrastination may lead you to avoid the situation. And when it's time to meet that person, you may not be able to save face. Avoidance increases depression and can contribute to a growing sense of fear and loneliness.

If you have identified yourself as a procrastinator, what should you do?

Be proactive. Keep a calendar and make a plan. Each night, list what you want to do the next day. Prioritize the list with the most important or difficult thing first. It might be a good idea to note the negative consequences that will arise if you fail to accomplish each task. End with the least important thing.

Take one step at a time. Finish the first task on your list before starting the second. If you try to do too many things at once, you may not end up doing any one of them well. The dopamine surge that you get from completing the first task will give you the momentum to do the next one.

Surround yourself with people who will keep you accountable. If you commit to do something, make sure you tell three or four of your friends, and ask them to check up on you. Realizing that you will be kept accountable for your promises by people you know and trust decreases the chance that you will procrastinate.

Almost everyone has procrastinated at one time or another, so don't feel too badly. However, this is an opportunity to change. Below you will find a procrastination checklist. I recommend taking a picture of this list and keeping it with you on your phone. If the answer to any of the questions is *yes*, it is an indication that you should not procrastinate, but instead, get to work.

Procrastination Checklist

Task I need to accomplish: _____

Please circle the corresponding answer: YES / NO

1. Will my procrastination result in negative consequences in my career, relationships, academics, or legal affairs?   Y   N

2. Do I lack motivation to accomplish this task?   Y   N

3. Is this task important to me or my family?   Y   N

4. Is this task important to my career?   Y   N

5. Am I procrastinating because of lack of knowledge or fear or embarrassment?   Y   N

6. If I wait a few days, will the task still need to be done?   Y   N

7. Will waiting keep me from being closer to my goals?   Y   N

If you marked any answer in the "yes" column, *go ahead and take steps to complete it.*

In these first chapters, I have outlined ways to make changes that positively affect personal development. As you identify and develop character traits and work on effective communication skills, self-examination will prove to be an important, fruitful activity. Once you are walking in forgiveness and making healthy and timely decisions, you are ready to turn your attention to the next section on professional development.

Section 2

Professional Development

Chapter 11: Your Purpose and Calling

W hat is your purpose? This is not usually an easy question to answer. My definition of purpose is that which you are destined for, what you are designed to do in this world now, at this time. Discovering your purpose requires you to be honest with yourself.

Your purpose is not what society or your parents or teachers expect of you. It is not a job or a title. What's more, your purpose is not static; it can change and transform over time. It is also not always comfortable. So, why do you have to answer this question for yourself? Why is it important that you understand your purpose?

A person without purpose is like a sheep without a shepherd or a stray dog without a home. When you know your purpose, you will be more fulfilled. You will have peace within, and you will not ever be bored. The continual and seemingly lifelong yearning for the next thing to accomplish will eventually stop. Dissatisfaction with daily life will diminish and you'll find contentment.

When I was in high school, I earned straight As. I thought doing well in class would fulfill me. It helped my parents, as they were able to brag about my schoolwork, but I was still unfulfilled. Then I thought, *Wait until I get to medical school! Then I will feel better*. But medical school came and went, and I was still unfulfilled. *Maybe when I became a physician?* But no, I still felt unfulfilled. What then?

As I mentioned above, your purpose is not necessarily a one-time, single thing. It may evolve, and mine certainly did. When I became a medical doctor, the constant yearning for the next thing, or something else, was still within me. It wasn't until I found my purpose and, later, my calling that I was able to feel contentment. This process began as I started to teach resident physicians at the hospital.

My teaching responsibilities with the residents were not going well. I was an impatient teacher, expecting too much too fast. So I took a step back and asked for feedback from my students as well as my colleagues. This helped me change strategies and develop better working relationships with both the residents and my colleagues. As a result, I was increasingly assigned to the more difficult students.

It became clear that my purpose was to teach and mentor young folks, believing in people when they had been cast out—seeing the best in everyone. I stumbled into my purpose without meaning to do so. I thought to myself, *Wouldn't it be nice to have guidance in finding your purpose without having to stumble upon it?*

Finding Your Purpose

Every person can find their purpose. In this section, I will offer questions and exercises that can help you do that. Knowledge of your own purpose at this time can profoundly affect your decisions and create new choices, providing better focus and confidence. The first step is to distinguish between potential, purpose, and calling.

Potential versus Purpose

It is important to differentiate purpose from potential. Your potential is everything you are capable of doing and includes all your gifts and abilities. These might be unformed talents, inclinations, likes, even dislikes, as well as abilities that you have developed and practiced. These can include the ability to play musical instruments or a particular physical skill you have developed. These are examples of the potential you have explored. For example, I can write, dance, play soccer, and act in plays. These are part of my potential.

However, purpose is what you are *meant* to do. It leads you into your destiny. For you to find your purpose, aspects of your potential often need to be sacrificed. This doesn't mean that you should give up every hobby or enjoyable pursuit, but it does require that you prioritize your actions. You must spend time enabling those attributes of yourself and developing skills that are in accordance with your purpose.

Purpose versus Calling

Since your purpose is what you are designed to do at this point in time, once you discover and are dedicated to it, the next step in the process is to find your calling. *Stay with your purpose, and life will lead you to your calling.*

I believe your calling is the Lord's intention in creating you. Your purpose helps guide you to who you will become in your calling. When your calling is clear, it allows you to become who you are supposed to be in this life. However, this process of finding your purpose and discerning your calling is not always clear-cut. There are many distractions that can interfere with finding the way to your purpose and calling. Here are some examples of this process and how distractions can dissuade and interfere with finding your purpose and calling.

The Sick Man

A pastor at a nearby church became aware that one of his congregants was troubled by almost-constant illness; it seemed that he was sick all the time. As soon as he was discharged from the hospital, he would contract another illness. The congregation was always praying for his health to improve, so finally the pastor asked him, "What is really going on?"

The answer was surprising. The sick man told the pastor that he had been called to be a missionary and travel to Africa as a young man. At a tent revival, he had been told that his calling was to be a minister, and that his work would be in Africa. He had been looking for his calling, and when he heard this, he was joyful and excited. After high school, he went to Bible school. And after his first year there, he fell in love and planned to get married.

He explained his calling to his wife; he told her that he had a special gift to become a minister in Africa. She seemed to agree at the time, but after the wedding, she resisted going to Africa, citing their recent marriage, and agreed to go in a few years. However, the next time he brought up his mission in Africa, his wife was pregnant and resisted traveling with him. As time went on, her stance continued. In the end, she told him it wasn't practical, and he didn't go to Africa.

"I was called to Africa, to do good works," the sick man said. "That's why there is no grace in my life. It's not the way it's supposed to be. I haven't been to Africa to fulfill my calling." Now in his 80s, the man was too old to fulfill his calling; his body could no longer do that work.

The Military Man

A former military man, now retired from active duty, felt called to go into the ministry and wanted to attend Bible school. As a young man, his grandparents had saved money for him to attend college, but he had gone to West Point, so they had gifted him the saved funds. He was well off financially and ready to start his studies at Bible school. However, he had conflicting emotions related to a woman he had met during his active-duty days.

She had problems with drugs and alcohol, and he had paid for her to attend a rehabilitation facility, which she was finishing. He was advised that it was not a good idea for her to move in with him, and he seemed to agree. But a few weeks later, he had asked her to move into his apartment, citing that she had nowhere else to go. She was staying in a separate bedroom and they were praying together.

Again, the man received strong advice: get her another apartment if you must, but don't get involved with her until she gets her act together! Intellectually, the military man agreed with the advice, but he didn't follow it. In a few months, the woman was pregnant. Since he was an honorable man, he married her.

However, this derailed his trajectory and the plans to which he felt called, for Bible school and the ministry were abandoned.

Distractions

Distractions might include uneasy relationships, such as in the examples above, an upcoming event, preoccupation with your work, or placing too much attention on input from your parents. Images in social media that suggest what people should do, how they should live, and what defines success are another distraction. Giving too much weight to social media and popular culture can interfere with your personal development, because *unnecessary and unrealistic expectations lead to confused actions*. Why should you want fit in when you are designed to stand out?

The phenomenon known as the "fear of missing out," or FOMO, leads people to undertake a multitude of activities, which may result in a lack of focus and feelings of emptiness as they are distracted from their purpose. This fuels uncertainty and bewilderment, making it more difficult to find your purpose and know your calling. Be aware of the influence of other people and their expectations. When you align with your purpose, your relationships will not drain you or make you feel lonely.

Find Your Purpose

A journal can really aid in figuring all this out, and every individual needs to do this for themselves. Here are some questions and exercises to help you find your purpose. Please take your time and answer them honestly, and remember that your answers may change over time.

1. What would you do for free? What profession or occupation or volunteer work would you gladly do without pay?

    Imagine waking up every morning and being excited about your work.

2. What agitates you? What irritates you and annoys you—gives you that "ugh" feeling? What are your trigger points?

    Whether it's injustice, child molestation, or politics, you must find out what that thing is that gets to your inner core. This is your passion. And your passion will lead you to your purpose. For example, when I see other people being taken advantage of, it affects my sense of inner calm.

3. If you could turn yourself into a superhero, what would your superpowers be?

    When I ask residents this question, their answer provides insight into what their passions are and creates a gateway to their purpose. They will choose something they can't do now, but that they want to do. It helps to understand what is possible. For example, one might wish for the ability to time travel to change past childhood traumas.

4. Do people praise you and tell you that you are good at specific tasks, work, or skills? What are they?

    For example, my daughter is very good at planning events. Even though this is not her job function, people always ask her to plan events. She also plans all of our travel together.

5. Do people tell you that you are a natural at certain activities? What are they?

For example, my wife, Lola, is a natural in prayer. She approaches every problem through prayer. She just goes into praying, and when she prays, most people feel something. Even when we visit places where they don't know her, she is singled out to pray.

6. Do you find yourself drawn to certain types of people? Which? Conversely, are there types of people who irritate you?

7. What types of people are drawn to you?

8. What grabs and sustains your attention?

9. What feedback do you get from people after you've done something?

10. What would motivate you to sacrifice some of your potential? For example, for what would you give up a lucrative job?

Try this: Note what you do, where you spend most of your time, and how you spend your money. This may not necessarily point to your purpose, but it could give you clues.

When finished, analyze your answers and see the correspondences. What answers overlap or connect? Do your answers lean toward a specific job or opportunity? If so, this may help guide you into your purpose and calling.

Know Yourself

A framework that might assist you in making sense of your answers to the questions above is the Japanese concept of *ikigai,* which translates in English to "life-purpose." The book *Ikigai: The Japanese Secret to a Long and Happy Life* by Hector Garcia and Francesc Miralles can help make sense of the statements, thoughts, and feelings that arose in the answers to the questions and exercises above.[2]

---

2. Hector Garcia and Francesc Miralles, *Ikigai: The Japanese Secret to a Long and Happy Life* (New York, NY: Penguin Life, 2017).

Use the four quadrant Venn diagram and examine your answers to the following four questions. Then analyze where they interlap. This intersection can help you understand your purpose and, eventually, your calling:

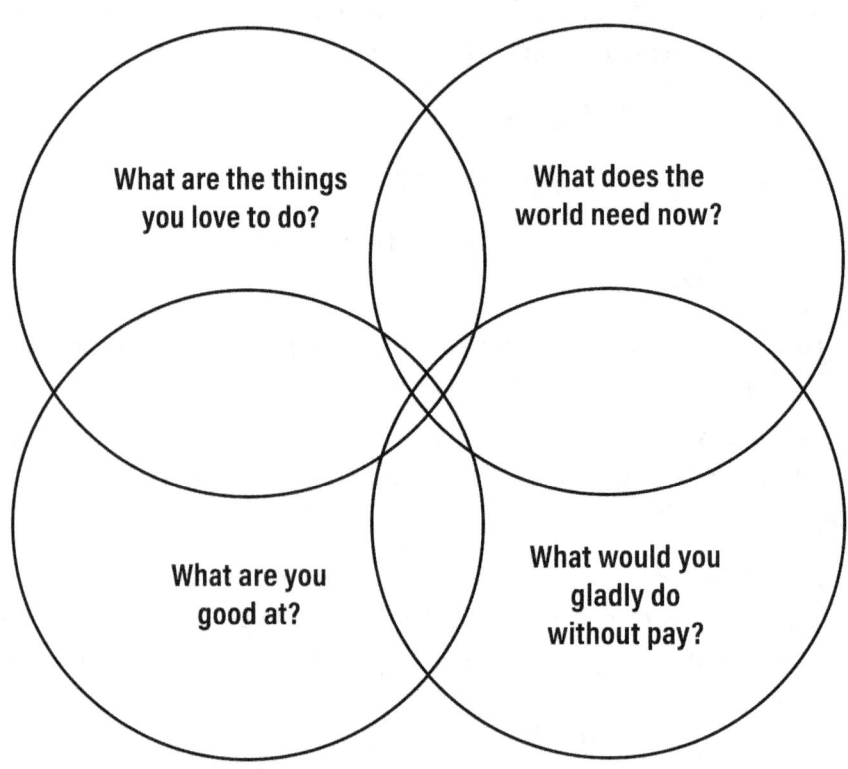

Limit the number of answers to each question by making sure they reflect authentic inner truths and the longings of your own heart. A purpose-driven life is a fulfilled life, so don't delay in doing the fundamental work of understanding your purpose.

If you can do this at an early age, you are less likely to waste time dabbling in unnecessary or harmful activities. However, it is a worthwhile inquiry at any age. Knowledge of your life purpose will help you achieve your potential in any profession you pursue. By aligning with the path for which you were created, you will find fulfillment in life and joy in your ability to serve others.

Chapter 12: Choosing a Career

People spend a third of their lives at work and another third in bed, sleeping. Sleeping is necessary and important to maintain health and energy. However, it is also important that the time spent at work be fulfilling and refreshing. So careful steps should be taken when choosing your career. Although it is quite possible to change careers, it's probably better to get it right the first time.

Usually when people are younger, their career choice is formed under the influence of parents, relatives like an aunt or uncle, or some other big figure—maybe even a movie star or sports celebrity. People can be motivated in choosing the right career by these external forces rather than investigating their own intrinsic values and qualities.

Outside Pressure

I grew up in a less industrialized country. In Nigeria, there were only a few careers that would be approved by most parents. You either became a doctor, an engineer, a nurse, a lawyer, or a teacher. The thinking was that your parents wanted job security and success for their children. However, they also wanted their child to be able to care for them when they were older. Nowadays, due to more economic complexity and job opportunities opening up around the globe, that requirement has waned, but not disappeared.

My uncle, who was a surgeon, decided that I was going to be a doctor when I was in ninth grade. He decided I would be a surgeon like him. My uncle said, "You are very good at science, so there's no reason for you to do anything other than become a physician." This came from my mother's younger brother and was totally supported by my parents. So the choice to become a physician was not my own. It eventually became so, but the original seed was planted by my uncle.

Despite my own experience with this, I am amazed at how much pressure is placed on the younger generation to choose a career. Our brains don't fully mature until the age of twenty-five, yet we expect seventeen and eighteen year olds, when first starting college, to choose a major degree program. It just doesn't make sense. The prefrontal cortex, which is the part of the brain involved with decision-making and maturity, is not developed by that time. So we should recognize that at this earlier stage, they can't fully make up their mind about what they want to do. So we should be careful when guiding them. Our ideas and beliefs about the future should not be imposed upon young people.

Internal Explorations

Society's timeline forces choices about the future on people in their teens and early twenties just the same. Therefore, they need to at least have an idea of what they want to do in terms of a career or, more importantly, what they do *not* want to do. This will help shape the choices made in terms of the school to attend, subjects to study, and people to shadow who can help aid their success.

Here are some steps that can serve as a guide to choosing a career:

1. **What do you do well?** Answer this question by listing your natural abilities, as well as the skills and abilities that other people see in you—things they ask you to do or express admiration over. Finally, what do you do that gives you satisfaction and joy?

As an example, I love human beings and interacting with people. I like to be helpful, and I am told that I am an optimistic person. So taking note of my ability, my nature, and my personality should inform my choice of career so that I don't have to struggle so much in whatever career choices I make.

When making a choice about your career, be careful not to base it on what others say. There are times when other people tell you that you are not good at certain things or complain about your work. It might depend on the individual person or situation, and there is also the possibility that you might improve and perform well later. When other people are negative about you or your capabilities, don't take it in a derogatory way. Use the experience to separate from the situation, go within yourself, and decide what is true. Are they people whom you trust? Are they trying to manipulate you or the situation? Is this an area in which you find personal satisfaction in spite of what others have said? Do you think you can do this job well anyway? If you find that the answers don't truly define you and your capabilities, you need to listen to yourself and push forward.

2. **What do you not do well?** What do you struggle to accomplish? Do other people tell you that you are not good at certain activities? Have you noticed that you react with frustration or distaste to any particular environment, task, or endeavor?

I am not a handy person. If you give me a screw and show me the hole it needs to go into as well as the manual, I still cannot put the screw in the hole. I remember trying to put a table together once. It was so stressful that after ten minutes, I was sweating heavily in an air-conditioned room. I gave up and got somebody else to do it. So for me to decide that I wanted to be a carpenter or builder would have been setting myself up for either failure or a very difficult and frustrating time.

3. **What is your personality like?** Are you an introvert or an extrovert? Do you like to work alone? Or in a group? Do you like to

always be the one in charge or are you good at taking orders? Do you collaborate with other people? Do you like structure, or are you more free floating? Do you operate with a "let's see how it goes" attitude or do you always make a plan?

It is important that your choice of career fits your personality type. There are a few free, online assessment tools available, including the Myers-Briggs personality type indicator and the Jungian type index. Or you can purchase a Harrison assessment, which gives you ranked choices for careers, as well as other indicators. This test is especially worthwhile if you are having trouble making a decision.

4. **What are deal breakers for you?** For example, some people do not like flying in an airplane, so for them to choose a career as a pilot or air host would just make their life more difficult. There is an argument that people who have a fear of flying may receive treatment for their anxiety by actually choosing such a career, but I don't suggest it! Even people who don't necessarily have a fear of flying don't always enjoy the experience, and if you don't do well with flying, you shouldn't be lining up to be a pilot.

This extends to other occupations too. What about sales, diplomacy, or working at a global company? If you don't like to travel, you may want to avoid these situations too. If you don't like to exert pressure on people, sales might not be a good choice for your career. Closely examine the skills and activities you cannot do, and for which you lack talent. Also exclude occupations or job situations that violate your core values.

Money and Benefits

In Chapter 15 of this book, "Money versus Time and Time versus Money," I discuss the difference between focusing on time and focusing on money. Money is important. You need it. You should choose a career that will give you enough resources to sustain yourself, your family, and your hobbies. Some jobs come with benefits, such as paid time off and retirement or 401K plans. How important are these types of benefits to you in choosing a career? If this is important to you, you will want to choose a career where the benefits are almost guaranteed versus a career where you won't get them.

Along similar lines, how much is it going to cost you to get that career? For example, if you want to be a lawyer or a psychologist, figure out how much you must pay (in money and in time) to get the necessary degrees and experience. If you want to pursue a medical specialty, such as neurosurgery, first be aware how many years are required for the residency, and often fellowships, before training is complete. Some careers, such as medicine and education, may give options for time spent in service programs that repay loans. Consider all the possibilities when it comes to the costs associated with your career choices.

Preferred Lifestyle

Next, consider what kind of lifestyle you want to lead. How does this affect your choice of career? Do you want a career where you spend most of your time at work? Or do you want a career with a more appropriate life/work balance? For example, if you choose to be a surgeon, you will spend most of your time in the operating room and little at home.

What are the alternatives? Do you want a career that gives you more flexibility? Do you want to be on call? Or do you want to be free after the workplace closes? Do you prefer to have your weekends free? These questions may tie into whether or not you want to have a family. Because if you don't want to have a family, your work sched-ule may be less important for you.

Workaholism

Many people are workaholics, despite having families. It's important to realize that the workaholic is getting fulfilled at work, but probably not at home. I've never seen somebody who was really happy at home become a workaholic. Work is an important form of validation and identity, and some people don't find these at home. People often tie their identity to their job. When I meet a guy at the gym, they often ask my name, and their next question is: "What do you do?"

This varies between individuals. Even if you are happy at home, you still must provide for your family, so everyone needs to work hard. A workaholic does this in an extreme manner. For example, let's say somebody has no mortgage or debt and is still working overtime every day. That suggests that the choice to work so hard and so much is about something other than providing for a family, or even enjoying the work.

Choosing to Change Careers

If you got on the wrong boat with your first career choice, it's never too late to change it. First, take all your previous experience into consideration. What worked for you and what didn't work for you? In other words, what did you like about your previous career and what didn't you like? As you choose another career, what skill level, education, and experience do you need to get into it?

Some people will go through these exercises, take a personality test, and still end up with five or more options. This is especially true for people who are multitalented and able to do several things very well. That can be a challenge. If you know you are good (or not) in one area, it's easy to make a choice, but if you are good at five different things, then how do you decide between them? You can create a list of options using the table on the next page to help you decide with more confidence.

Rank your career choices. Complete the provided tables of pros and cons or write these in a journal or notebook if you need more space, and consider what we've talked about: values, lifestyle, salary, benefits, and so on.

Career Choice:		Career Choice:		Career Choice:	
PRO	CON	PRO	CON	PRO	CON

Reflecting on these tables may help you decide, but if you are still unsure between two or three careers, just jump into one and see. You will soon be able to tell whether it's right. Or you may want to work at two part-time jobs that span these careers so you can determine which one you like most. That might be a good way to finally choose.

For example, let's say someone wants to do both nursing and acting. They work during the week as a nurse, getting a regular salary and benefits, while on evenings and weekends, they start acting in plays. This way they can see which career is actually giving them the most satisfaction, and which one should be the focus. In the field of medicine, there are a few set career options for those who cannot make up their mind. For example, you can choose to combine a residency in psychiatry and neurology or pediatrics and pediatric psychiatry. These are some of the most common ones. These combinations require a longer amount of time spent to train in both specialties, and you can practice in both specialties when you are finished. However, going through the process on both allows people to see where they belong, and they usually gravitate to one job more than the other.

Other useful techniques to employ include shadowing people while they work and networking. When shadowing, you can observe different job functions and work environments and get a chance to ask questions. Networking is extremely valuable when it comes to getting useful information about various career paths. Ask direct questions, such as:

- What do you like about your job?
- What don't you like about your job?
- What would you do differently?

I often tell medical students that they should go around and ask the attending physicians about their specialties. Ask them questions! They will tell you if it is worth it or not. They will share what they think would make things better. They will share their passion for the medical field. They will share what they love and what they hate as well as what they tolerate.

Recently, an oncologist told me that he couldn't wait to retire. My reaction was that if you are in the right job and good at it, you would not be thinking of retirement. He was not that close to retirement age. What brought on this lack of fulfillment was his inadequate research before choosing his career. He became overwhelmed by the expectations of the job and burnt out. He lost his passion as the pressures of the job ate away at his joy.

Evaluating Your Career Choice

If you wake and can't wait to get to work, that's a good sign. You are probably in the right profession. But if you wake up thinking negatively about going into work, you should start looking for another career.

For example, I know a guy who digs swimming pools. It is how he makes his living, but it's not really a job to him. He loves being outside and loves digging stuff up. He chose a great career and is doing what he loves and getting paid for it. As you progress through your working life, revisit these guidelines for choosing a career. Ask yourself these questions:

- What are your career goals?
- What are your values?
- What are your interests and skills?

Ask yourself these questions regularly, and at the end of day you will be able to discover where you should be and who you are. This information will help you decide which career to pursue, whether your present career is fulfilling, and if you should make a change.

Chapter 13: How to Ace Your Interview

A job interview goes beyond a two-way conversation. It involves being compatible with the mission and culture of the place.

No matter what, chances are that you will have to do an interview at some point. Jobs, volunteer positions, and school admissions often require one. I compare an upcoming interview with going into a battle. You are trying to win, so it is not wise to go into battle without adequate preparation. This chapter contains the necessary strategies for preparing to go into the interview arena.

Preparation

First, know your opponents. Let's say you are interviewing for a job. The battle is between you, the institution where you want to work, and the other job seekers—your competition for the position. Most of the time, you are not the only candidate. Give yourself the best chance of winning the battle by taking the time to adequately prepare.

Do your research. Know the institution and what it represents; learn about its mission, values, beliefs, and future direction. This is easily accomplished by searching the Internet for the institution and talking to people who currently work there, as well as former employees.

It is also important to find out about the people who are going to conduct the interview. This strategy is easier with the help of search engines. When interviewing within medical or academic fields, learn not only about the people on the interview panel, but also read about their research ideas and scan through their publications. This will be very helpful during the interview.

The last strategy—knowing your competition—may not be so easy. The institution may not disclose the names of the other applicants. No matter, it's safest to imagine that the other applicants are better than you. That gives you the opportunity to try harder. This pushes you to identify your areas of strength and excellence, so you can bring them into the battle.

Practice

The next strategy for the battle is to practice what you have to say. Practice with a mirror or set up a mock interview with friends. Have them throw questions at you, so you can practice your responses. When you practice, you can make mistakes. If you have people listening, they will pick up on your mistakes and give feedback so you can practice again. If friends are not available, record yourself practicing for the interview. Next, show the video to people who are close to you and ask for their comments and evaluations. Invite them to give feedback. For your convenience, I've included some practice questions at the end of the chapter.

If there is a recruiter involved in finding applicants for the position, it may help to talk to them too. They have experience with what worked in the past and may be able to advise you on a strategy that will increase your chances. If recruiters are working to fill the position, they may be interested in coaching and encouraging you, because this helps them too.

The Day of the Interview

It's the big day! Recognize that the interview starts before you leave your home. You need to be mentally sharp and strong. Don't do anything that will stress you out the night before the interview. Avoid quarrels or heated discussions that could linger in your mind and affect your focus.

Don't go out and party all night! A good night's sleep goes a long way to help you feel refreshed. Have a good breakfast—something light that won't make you feel sleepy. If you are a coffee drinker, try not to drink too much; you don't want to interrupt the interview by having to go to the bathroom.

If the interview is out of town, be there at least a day before and get familiar with the area. You don't want to be late. If you run into people who work at the institution, ask them about it. That way if the interviewers ask you how much you know about them, you can preface the answer with, "I talked to a few people last night, and…." This can pull a lot of weight in terms of your chances. It shows that you are really interested in the place and have taken the time to arrive early and investigate.

Your dress is important. Study the institution and dress accordingly. If you are planning for a job as an executive, you would wear business attire and look nice. Don't wear jeans and flip flops. However, if you apply for a blue-collar job, you don't need to wear a suit or tie. Your dress should match the position for which you apply. Do not look sloppy, and also, do not wear strong perfume or deodorant. Some people may be allergic.

During the Interview

In most cases, it is important to make good eye contact. However, in some non-Western cultures, maintaining eye contact is considered rude. So be sure to understand the culture where you are interviewing. However, if you don't make good eye contact in Western societies, it is perceived as a lack of confidence. In fact, if you are being interviewed by a group of people, you should make eye contact with *everyone in the group.*

Once the interview begins, do not be afraid to lead the conversation; in fact, you should take control. Start with questions or comments discussing the mission and vision of the company. At this point, you should have familiarized yourself with the company's website to even bring up the company's values and that's a mark in your favor. Be articulate about how you can help and how you see yourself fitting into the bigger picture. Leading the conversation also gives you the opportunity to talk about your accomplishments. Most people are shy about this; however, employers respect you more if you're confident and able to talk about your achievements.

For example, let's say there is a resident trying to get a job in an institution that is dedicated to building its services for women. If this resident is strong in that area, they can make a statement such as, "I understand that one of your areas of future development is in women's health. That's something I am excited about because I have a lot of experience in that area." That may pique their interest, causing them to ask about those experiences. Guiding the conversation in this way gives you a chance to talk about your strengths, providing fortunate opportunities to reveal your expertise.

I recommend writing down your accomplishments before the interview. In fact, you can even print a copy of your accomplishments and achievements for yourself and your interviewers. This is different from your CV or resume, which they may or may not have had the opportunity to read. Bring a page with bullet points showing what you've achieved and what you can bring to the company.

Even though you should take charge of the conversation, do not interrupt the interviewers. Don't cut people off when they are asking a question. This can be a sign of either anxiety or overconfidence and can come across as being too abrupt. Be sure to wait your turn. If you don't understand a question, do not try to answer the question you think they are asking. Stop and have them repeat the question or repeat the question back to them to make sure you understand what they are asking. Avoid using slang, such as "you know" or "like." It's not appropriate in this setting.

Further, be ready to be challenged during the interview. For example, if you have a bad reference or if you left a previous job, be ready to acknowledge the *real reason* why you left. Don't be defensive.

Focus on what you will bring to the institution, rather than what the institution will give you. Sell yourself, not arrogantly, but confidently. This is why I suggest that you practice for the interview. Practicing builds you up internally for the give-and-take that characterizes the conversation you are about to have. It allows you to focus better.

Additionally, it's important not to focus too much on the salary or the benefits. You do not have to discuss that before an offer is made. However, they may ask you about salary expectations. I like to answer this by saying, "I know you will be fair. I know what the going rate is for my position, and I believe you will give me the offer I deserve." The advantage of this strategy is in not revealing the salary figure you had in mind. Once you have stated a number, if they were going to offer you more, you have already boxed yourself in. If they offer a higher salary, that's a win for you. The disadvantage of this strategy is that they might offer you a much lower salary than you want. Then you have to work to increase the offer. Strategies for negotiation are covered in the next chapter.

During the interview, remember the main discussion points that came up with each interviewer. Mentally take note of the areas that energize or light up the interviewers. This will be the focus of the letter you write to thank them after the interview.

Practice Interview Questions

Here are some questions that are commonly asked during interviews, but you can be sure that you will be asked more questions than those listed here.

- What are your strengths and weaknesses?
- What will you bring to this institution?
- How do you get along with your coworkers and supervisors?
- How well do you take correction and criticism?
- What is the most interesting or most devastating thing that has ever happened to you?
- How would your coworkers describe you?
- Why did you leave your last job?
- If I call one of your references, what will they say about you?
- What do people like (and don't like) about you?
- What makes you uncomfortable?
- How do you react to pressure? How do you respond to pressure?
- What's your greatest disappointment?

Answering questions about your strengths and weaknesses is tricky. It's easy to highlight your strengths and tell interviewers about what you do well. For example, you might mention your organizational skills or how you get along with people. However, when it comes to questions about weaknesses, you want to answer in such a way that you turn those weaknesses into strengths.

It's a fine balance.

Here's a personal example of how I have answered a question about my weaknesses. I said, "I am working on the ability to say no more often. In the past, I wasn't very good at saying no, which made me take on more responsibilities than my colleagues. But I learned that when I say no, I can focus on the details of my assigned job and perform better." On one hand that's a weakness, but I've also told them I am going to work hard and that I don't whine.

Afterward

It is important to follow up soon after the interview. In fact, I recommend writing a thank you note immediately after the interview, so the conversations are still fresh in your mind. It doesn't have to be an essay, just a simple letter of thanks. Here's an example.

> Thank you for your time. I enjoyed the discussion we had during the interview, especially when you were re-ferring to _____. (This is where you bring up areas where the interviewers became excited or enthused. Be sure to share your opinion about that subject.)

Use a positive tone in your thank you note. Indicate that you are excited to join the institution, and rephrase what you are going to bring to the table. If you want to compliment one of the interviewers, be specific. Be careful not to appear insincere. I think using email is less personal than a handwritten note; however, it is also possible to write a short email first, and then follow with a handwritten note.

Chapter 14: Negotiations for Compensation

A while ago, I was changing positions within the same healthcare system. Even though I was changing jobs, I was not relocating. During the interview for my new position, I asked to be compensated with relocation expenses. To my surprise, my interviewer said, "I can only give you $5,000." I countered with $20,000 and we settled at $10,000. I ended up receiving "free" money that I definitely would not have received if I had not requested it.

The majority of people are skeptical, worried, and anxious about negotiation. However, if you do your homework and have the right facts, the process of negotiation can benefit you greatly. It doesn't matter whether you're looking for a new job or want a raise at your current job, you should constantly be negotiating.

However, it is difficult to negotiate unless you know your true worth. Another difficulty is not knowing what the competition will pay you. The primary reason people do not negotiate is that it can provoke anxiety or that they fear rejection. Imagine not negotiating your salary and finding out six months later that someone less qualified is getting paid significantly more. This is frustrating. If you feel undervalued, it can ultimately lead to performing your duties inadequately and experiencing low morale. Therefore, this is another area to consider. Some of the content in this chapter overlaps with the one you just read, but consider this as further, and slightly different, applications of those principles.

Tips for Negotiating Properly

Know Your Worth

Knowing what you're worth is of paramount importance. You must not only know what you're worth, you should also not be shy in expressing it. You can find out your monetary worth by simply Googling people who are similar to you in terms of education, academic achievement, and work experience. Find out how much they are making in both your geographic area and your industry or specialization. This step is crucial. Do not want to wait until the interview to do this research.

You may also talk to professional recruiters or search for jobs online to see how much they pay. There are a few websites, including Salary. com or Payscale.com, that give an average value for how much you should be making in a particular industry and location. Indeed.com and Glassdoor.com are other resources to discover what people are earning in the type of position you seek.

Do Not Focus Only on Money

Most salary jobs come with benefits, and people tend to focus on this aspect. Unfortunately, when thinking about the salary, they may not consider the hours that are required to complete their work. For example, if you make $80,000 a year and you have to work eighty hours a week, it sounds like a $65,000 yearly salary working forty hours a week is a much better deal. You can use the rest of your time for recreation, spending time with your family, learning a new hobby, or even making extra cash by signing up for extra shifts.

Identify what is good for you, and consider your values instead of only considering the money. Also, find out the range of benefits they provide. Do they contribute to a 401K? What is the matching rate? How many days of paid vacation do you get? How many paid sick days do you get? Are there opportunities for self-improvement or continuing education? Are payments available for continuing education? Is there an opportunity for a sabbatical? The most important thing to negotiate is time, not necessarily money.

Be Willing to Walk Away

A deal that you feel too strongly about is already a bad deal and you must be willing to walk away from any deal. This is not always easy! Always have alternative options. Assuming you want a job in a particular industry, you should have alternative interviews lined up too. When you have other options, you will not be desperate or disappointed if one does not work out. The control is then in your hands and it will make it easier to walk away from acceptable offers that do not provide you with what you want. However, you should be a little flexible.

Do Your Research

Learning about the company will help determine what you need to bring to the table. You must do enough research to determine how your skills, abilities, and knowledge will add value to the company. When interviewing, do not be shy, but also do not exaggerate or fabricate your skills, experience, or what you're capable of. It will not look good if you get hired but cannot follow through on your promises and the company's expectations.

Timing Is Everything

You may not always have this option, but you should consider applying for a job or a new position when your current company has an opening for a position in which you're interested. Someone may have just retired or left the position, providing you with the perfect opportunity to either ask for a raise or move into the vacant position. You will most likely need to demonstrate more responsibility to show you are qualified for the new role.

Be Confident

I recommend the initial negotiation be done by email, as this reduces the anxiety that may come from a face-to-face interaction. If you must negotiate with company executives, you may be able to articulate your thoughts better in this fashion. However, at some point you'll most likely have to talk to the person or interviewer face to face. On the day of the interview, you should dress for the job you want. This includes dressing appropriately, making sure you are adequately groomed, and walking with confidence.

If you have a choice about when to do the meeting or interview, make it later in the week. The later in the week, the better. I suggest setting the interview for a Thursday or a Friday. During the beginning of the week, supervisors and managers may be tougher because they are more focused, sharper, and more likely to identify your flaws or deficiencies. These same professionals are more likely to be in a better mood when the week is winding down and the weekend is approaching.

Don't Be the First to Name a Number

Some employers may ask how much money you are looking for, and there are two schools of thought on this. Some people think you should shoot for a higher number because they believe if they ask for something ridiculously high, the number will be lowered to what they actually want. An example of this tactic is asking for $50,000 if you want to make $40,000 a year, knowing that your potential employers will drag the number down.

As previously mentioned, I favor a different approach, where you say something like, "I've done my research, so I know how much I'm worth. I know how much people with my level of education and experience get paid, and I trust you'll be fair." The advantage of this technique is that they may offer you a number which is much higher than you were thinking. If you had started with a number lower than what they planned to offer, you would have already lost a significant amount of money. Those who are in favor of starting high believe that employers will try to bring your salary down, but if you are first offered a number higher than you're expecting, you've already won.

Do Not Focus on Solely on Your Personal Needs

You want to pay attention to the progress of the company, not necessarily what is good for you. Those hiring you want to know that you not only care about making money for yourself, but also are invested in the goals of the company or organization.

Be Prepared to Ask Questions

The potential employers will expect you to ask questions. If you've done your research thoroughly, you can ask questions that show your interest in the progress of the company. "How do you think my knowledge in IT will be useful to the latest innovations of the company?" "How does the rehab department impact the vision of the entire company?"

Negotiations Do Not Have to Be a One-Time Deal

After finishing your first interview, continue to negotiate via email. After emailing your interviewers to thank them for their time, bring up what was discussed in the interview and how you will add value to their company. This email could end with you stating, "I have thought about it, and if you agree to my request of $50,000 a year, that would be a good motivating factor for me to decline my other job offer."

Don't Forget to Ask for "Extras"

Do not forget to ask for things like relocation reimbursement, sign-on bonuses, and other perks. Remember, if you don't ask, the answer is already no.

Remember That They Are Using You

Lastly, when you're negotiating you must have the mindset that the people on the other side of the table *want to take advantage of you*; they want to use you. This mindset makes you more decisive and persistent in your negotiations.

Negotiations for compensation can be scary, but with these strategies, anxiety will be decreased. Therefore, find out what workers in your geographic and professional area earn, demonstrate the caliber of your contributions, and build your own confidence about what you will bring to the institution. Knowing your worth and being confident can significantly increase your chances of making more money or getting the promotion you desire, but please remember that money or salary is just one part of the compensation you need to negotiate. Benefits like paid time off, continuing education opportunities, 401K matching contributions, and travel bonuses are others. There is also the balance between work time and time away from work. These are all factors that add value to the overall compensation that comes with the position, and they should all be considered in addition to the money.

Chapter 15: Money versus Time and Time versus Money

We've all heard that "time is money," but I think a more accurate statement is "time is life."

When I was in the U.K. as a resident physician, I was a father of young children. I also had to take my share of the on-call schedule. The on-call schedule was from 5 p.m. on a Friday until 9 a.m. on the following Monday. After the call, I had to continue working until Monday at 5 p.m. So, essentially, I was away from my family from 5 p.m. Friday until 5 p.m. Monday. At that time, I had two children, ages one and two years old, and a wife who needed me. I wanted to spend time with my children and my family, but I couldn't quit my job as a resident! That wouldn't get me anywhere, so I decided to take my family to the call room for the weekend.

This was a way I could spend time with my family and still take care of the patients who needed me in the hospital. Granted, it wasn't the best-case scenario for spending time with my family, but at least I could see them when I wasn't busy with hospital business. I spent time with them between patient visits. Looking back, I think I made the best choice. The other option was not to see them for three nights and four days. In this scenario, I had to find a balance between time and money.

Money versus Time

That experience kept me thinking about the value of money versus time. It's not the same for everyone. This chapter is going to address these concepts and give guidance on how to determine priority and balance over time and money. For example, negotiating for money versus time might depend on one's stage of life. If you are younger and don't have a family, and you also don't have a lot of hobbies, you may want to negotiate for more money. But if you are getting older and have a family with whom you want to spend time, negotiating for more time makes more sense. Ideally, it's nice to get more money *and* more time, but that's not always realistic.

You can always make more money, but time is limited and finite; you only have enough. Most often, you can convert time to money through working and applying yourself in activities that earn payment. However, you can't really convert money into time. There are ways to use money to buy time through negotiating with your workplace or altering your personal schedule to get more free time. Conversely, if you need more money, you can always convert that time back into money.

When I moved to the U.S., I was in my late twenties. I used to ask people I'd meet who were in their forties and fifties (I talked with about 100 people) if they had any regrets. The majority said they wished they had spent more time with their wife or children. Very few regretted not making enough money. Most of them thought they had lost time with their family—time that could never be regained. I also interviewed a few people who were dying. I asked them about their greatest regret. Nobody ever said they wished they'd worked for another degree or made another million. Their regret always centered on time—time with their loved ones.

So I vowed that I would never have those regrets. Time may be money, but if it's considered more closely, time is life. If you are wasting your time, you are wasting your life. Don't let that happen.

Time versus Money

The value of time remains constant because you can only do so much in a certain amount of time, unless you get very efficient with how much you accomplish. However, it's not easy to enumerate. You can count how much money you have, but you don't know how much time you will have. I can look at my bank account and say I have ten million dollars, but I can't say that I have fifty more years to live with any assurance. Additionally, money loses value over time due to inflation. When you are making the decision to amass wealth, you have to realize that over the next few years that money will lose value, unless you invest it in a way that generates income.

While it may look like I'm not rooting for more money, just more time, there are two scenarios in my mind whereby you may value having more money over more time. The first scenario is when you are young and strong. At that time in your life, you can make more money in a short period of time. If you use this money to generate more income, then you can eventually free yourself and have time to enjoy the money. There is absolutely no point in spending all your time making money for someone else to enjoy. The second scenario is for people who want power. Sometimes money can buy you power, or the illusion of holding power.

One thing to keep in mind, however, is that it's generally easier in our society to assign value to money and harder to assign a value to our time.

Let's say I want to go to Florida for vacation. I could drive, which would take me a whole day, or I could fly, which would take three to five hours. Depending on how valuable I consider my time to be, it might be cheaper for me to fly. However, if I want to enjoy the scenery on a road trip and consider exploring the South as I drive to Florida, a pleasant use of time, it is not better to fly. So everyone must examine their own evaluation of time.

Another example is when it comes to making repairs. I am not very handy. If you give me two pieces to glue together, I can find a way to mess that up. So if I buy something in the store that needs to be assembled, it is better for me, financially and emotionally, to pay somebody to assemble the item for me. It doesn't matter that the box says "Do It Yourself" in large, red letters. If I try to do it myself, I'll get frustrated, angry, and, eventually, in trouble with my wife because I messed it up. I know my limitations. In my case, I am simply not good at building things. That's where money comes in. It buys me some non-stressful time that I can use to do something I enjoy. The money spent is worth the hours and frustration I would have been struggling with putting that table or bicycle together, a process for which I have no talent whatsoever. If I choose, I could have even used that allotted time to make more money.

In general, if you are older and you have a reasonable amount of savings, time becomes more valuable than money. A 2010 study at Princeton University found that emotional well-being leveled off with an annual income of $75,000.[3] When the respondents earned more than that, their everyday emotional experiences did not improve. In other words, they were not necessarily happier or more fulfilled because they made a lot of money.

We may even have to resist the urge to make more and more money, because the urge is always there. Even though you have a lot of money, you may still think you need more. Money is one of the few things we don't get tired of. We get tired of too much food or exercise. We can drink too much water or alcohol, but I've never heard anyone say, "Oh, no! I have too much money!" There is no feedback mechanism for too

---

3. Daniel Kahneman and Angus Deaton, "High Income Improves Evaluation of Life but Not Emotional Well-Being," Princeton University, August 4, 2010, https://www.princeton.edu/~deaton/downloads/deaton_kahneman_high_income_improves_evaluation_August2010.pdf.

much money. Instead, ask yourself: what do I need now? Can I get this time back? Would more money buy me time with my family?

Conclusion

The decision to prize time over money, or vice versa, is multi-factorial and personal. Ask yourself the following questions and consider these guidelines, which may help in making decisions about time versus money.

1. What stage of life am I in? Younger? Older? Do I have family to share my time with? How much income do I have now? Do I have enough to take a step back and enjoy life? Or do I need to invest in my job and make more money now in order to have the quality time that I want in the future? How much money do I really need?

2. Do I have enough or do I need more? Consider all options carefully. Do I actually need that boat or the cottage on the lake or a second home in Florida? How much time will I spend there? Will it add to my stress to pay more bills and deal with security expenses? Do I really *need* that? Or do I just want it? If you have enough, you have to ask yourself if you need more. If you don't need more, you don't need to work more or get that extra job. You can be fulfilled with what you have.

3. What are your values in terms of your material objects, hobbies, and self-development? That's a loaded question. Do you need more material things? Because if you do, you need more money. However, you may not. Do you want more time to develop hobbies, like learning to play the piano or guitar? If you do, you need more time. If you want to develop yourself in any way, maybe learn another life skill, such as how to swim or ski, it all takes time. Most self-development requires a time commitment. Don't get another job if you want this because those activities all need time. That's the bottom line.

4. If you sacrifice time now to make more money, is that going to translate into having more time in the future to do what you want to do? On the other hand, if you take time right now at this stage in your life, are you going to run out of money? These decisions are not necessarily easy and shouldn't be made in a hurry.

When I was a resident on call in the U.K. taking my family to the hospital for the weekend, I was finding a way to make money and spend time with family. My kids loved it and have always remembered it as a positive experience. When my son was around ten, he even asked to go along with me to the hospital when I was on-call. We spent time together and stayed overnight in the call room. Through creative problem-solving, I was able to stay on track with my career as a resident and spend precious time with my wife and young children. I think I made the best decision for the use of my time at that point of my life.

Chapter 16: A Four-Day Work Week

W hy do we need a four-day work week? Everybody seems to complain about having too short of a weekend. One guy told me, "If you can get the government to give us a three-day weekend, I will work for you!" Pilot studies have shown that workers can maintain one hundred percent of their normal productivity on a four-day schedule.

In Iceland, there was a study on the four-day work week. Workers reduced their hours to 35 or 36 hours a week. It was determined that productivity remained the same or improved.

The Advantages

The advantages of a four-day work week include increased productivity. When people know that they have only four days to get the work done, they are more likely to work harder. This is contrary to conventional thinking that you will get more work done over a period of five days, but all the studies show that we achieve greater productivity with a four-day work week.

In addition, there are cost savings. Employees don't have to travel to work five days a week. This saves travel expenses. When they go to the office four days a week, there may be a savings in energy costs for the workplace. Heat and air conditioning can be either turned down or off, depending on the weather and type of workplace. There may be less use of electricity, and cleaning services can also be reduced. Alternatively, employers may be able to use the workplace facility as another source of income, renting out the space for a day or utilizing it for another aspect of their overall business.

Employee retention is also better with a four-day work week. Employees are more rested with three days off during the week. They approach their work with more energy, and there is potential for achieving a better work/life balance. In other words, employees have more time for their families, hobbies, and other pursuits. With a greater chance to focus on themselves as a whole person, everybody in their community benefits.

The Disadvantages

There could be some disadvantages to working four days a week. One of the main challenges is the schedule. In workplaces where coverage is needed, staff must cover the fifth day. However, many employees prefer to have one day off midweek, and would rather take Monday off over Friday. The idea of working four days a week is usually very appealing to employees, and so it will probably be fairly simple to determine the work schedule.

Another downside is that sometimes putting so much pressure on yourself, or another employee, for those four days can lead to more stress. If this is the case, carefully examine the expectations around your deadlines and workloads. Are they realistic? Also, take a look at the way the work week is scheduled; that may also have an impact on stress.

Scheduling the Four-Day Work Week

Let's examine the schedule. As an employee, what would you prefer? You might assume there would be four ten-hour days. However, I advocate that you plan to work eight-hour days without any reduction in pay, so the real question is this: How can a person work thirty-two hours and get paid for forty hours and still accomplish the job at hand?

Switching to a four-day work week will meet the overall production and revenue goals of the business because of the increased motivation and productivity on the part of employees, reduced costs to the workplace facility, and better employee retention, which in turn reduces hiring and training expenses. In other words, you should be able to schedule four eight-hour days and retain the same salary you earned previously working forty hours a week.

However, if you are required to work ten-hour days, be sure to use those last two hours of the day to perform administrative tasks. This is especially true in the "caring" professions, such as medical professionals, nurse practitioners, and therapists. This time is best for administrative or charting tasks. This makes great sense for healthcare professionals. Why not get paid for charting, rather than performing this work outside of your regular work hours?

Junior physicians and some other healthcare professionals don't usually have much flexibility or vacation during training, but most senior physicians and practitioners take regular vacations. I recommend vacation every six weeks. It doesn't have to be complicated. Just get out and refresh yourself. However, in the healthcare field, the first call is to the patient, so most physicians will abandon their vacation, or even their sick days, if there is need. It's important to realize that this has to become more balanced. Doctors and the like are responsible for their patients, but at the same time, they must take care of themselves first to perform that responsibility well.

Getting paid for forty hours and working thirty-two is the goal that employees should aim for by increasing their efficiency. When people work a four-day weekly schedule, I strongly recommend that they take a Tuesday or Friday off. The reason I recommend Tuesday is that most public holidays fall on Mondays, so that builds in a *four-day weekend* for public holidays. Even so, choosing to take Friday off means they always get a three-day weekend. Other employees prefer a midweek break. This is good for running errands, household tasks, and may create more free time on the two-day weekends.

An Employer's Perspective

Employers may be asking themselves, *How will this be advantageous for me?* It increases the motivation to get the work done well on the part of your employees. You can also sell the four-day week and use it for recruitment. *People will want to work for you.* There are also potential savings in workspace and energy bills. Paradoxically, there ends up being less downtime for employees because they tend to work more efficiently in four days than they do in five. As a result of having three days off a week, they are likely to take fewer sick days.

Microsoft experimented in one of their Japanese offices by testing a four-day work week for one month. The Work-Life Choice Challenge Summer 2019 gave employees Fridays off in August. There was no decrease in pay. The results were very positive. Productivity increased by forty percent. Employees were happier too. An additional feature of the experiment was extra vacation pay, which was provided along with the encouragement to spend the time with family.

Another potential advantage of scheduling four days a week for your business is the positive ecological benefit in reduction of environmental pollution. Using less gas and energy in the office saves in energy bills and contributes to an overall reduction in the amount of pollution caused by that energy use.

A disadvantage for employers might be in the area of scheduling and coverage. If an employee requests, and gets, a four-day work week, other employees will want to do the same. As an employer, you have to figure out a fair balance. If your business must remain staffed five or more days a week, perhaps you can give employees their free day on different days. As an employer myself, I think the advantages outweigh the disadvantages.

Requesting a Four-Day Work Week

You can't just wish for it though; you have to ask for it. Therefore, you need to know what and how to ask.

The first thing is do your own work very well. Be ready to show productivity data to your employer when you ask about a four-day work week. Explain that it would not affect your productivity but actually increase it.

If you are already on a five-day work week, you have to make sure there are no current complaints about your work. You need to do a stellar job, be very efficient, and show that you can finish your work in a quality manner. Do this for some time. This is the data you are going to use when asking for reduced time.

Once there are no complaints about your work and you finish it on time, you have to address the issue head-on. An example would be to say, "I can do this in eight hours instead of ten." If your employer is reluctant, you can suggest trying it for the next three months. Then you can use those three months to both increase your productivity and collect data along the way that shows *how* you are more productive.

Use those three months to track your accomplishments. Share your methods for tracking this data with your employer. That way they know you are being upfront and transparent. It also shows that you are not afraid of them tracking you. Another master stroke is to explain to your employer the advantages of the four-day work week, showing solutions to any problems that may arise:

- "You may think you will have a problem with scheduling, but this is how I'm going to address that."
- "This is my suggestion for solving that potential problem."

Make it easy for the employer to say yes. Of course, there is a chance that the employer will say no. And if that happens, don't quit! Just work harder and ask again in six months. By working harder, I mean remain a good employee. Don't grumble. And ask again. All the residents and medical students whom I have mentored are scheduling four-day work weeks, and they always come back to thank me.

The benefit of a four-day work week is to get more time for yourself and your family. However, should you need more money, you can still use the extra day to get another position or two. This is also good time for more training and education or to explore hobbies. There are so many things one can do with one extra day a week. Bottom line: When you have more time for yourself and your family, you approach your work refreshed. It's more enjoyable. You are not as tired. You can only keep running on full—not empty.

Chapter 17: Debt and Other Matters

M ost teenagers are not very mature, so it is not uncommon for banks to take advantage of them and lure them with credit or debit cards. My banker called one day and wanted to know how we had trained our children to turn down credit cards. He had called my son and offered him a debit card, and my son said no. However, not everybody is privileged to know that you have to teach your children to say no. Inevitably, some people get into debt.

Credit Card Debt

The most difficult kind of debt to pay off is credit card debt. If you check the APR (the percentage of interest) on most credit cards, it is easily around twenty-one percent to thirty percent, and sometimes higher. If you are a careful and thoughtful spender who is able to pay *off* your credit card bills by the end of the month, then keeping one or two credit cards is a reasonable option for you. However, if you feel like your spending is out of control or you cannot keep track of where your money is going, then reducing your credit cards to nothing should be your only option.

In case you did not know, credit card companies have strategies to set you up to miss your payments. For instance, they recommend you only pay the minimum payment, which, depending on how much you owe, may take the rest of your life. If you do that every month and figure in that high interest rate, in the end, you might pay for that item three times over. Meanwhile, they bombard you with "deals" that look great on a daily basis. They're hard to resist. They entice you with *free* airline miles, *free* hotel stays, cash back, and other perks. Why would they want to give you free stuff? It's because they know they've got you.

If you find yourself sucked into deep credit card debt, do not give up; there's hope. The first thing you need to do is plastic surgery and *cut up all your credit cards*. Then pay the whole amount on the card with the smallest balance, while continuing to pay the minimum payments on the other credit cards. Once the one with the lowest balance is paid off, then start paying off the next one with the smallest balance, until all your credit card balances are at zero. Once you have paid them off, do not make the mistake of getting another one.

Another thing you can do to get out of debt quickly is to spend less. Use the table on the following page to help you keep a spending diary and trace how you use your money.

"Just as the rich rule the poor, so the borrower is
servant to the lender."
—Proverbs 22:7

Monthly Expenses			
Recurring (Necessary to Live)		**Non-Recurring (Splurging)**	
Mortgage/Rent		Eating Out	
Groceries		Gifts	
Car Expenses		Fun Shopping	
Insurance(s)		Hobbies	
Utilities		Entertainment	
Health Expenses		Unexpected Expenses	
Other:		Other:	
Total Recurring Expenses	$_____	**Total *Non*-Recurring Expenses**	$_____

Now let's do some math:

Total Monthly Income $_____

Subtract the Recurring Monthly Expenses $_____

Subtract the *Non*-Recurring Monthly Expenses $_____

The remainder = Monthly Savings $_____

Look at the "Non-Recurring" column—what part of your spending do you consider wasteful? What could be cut back or cut out? It could be cutting out that cup of coffee at a nearby drive-through every morning on the way to work, going out to eat too often, or habitually buying something you can easily take care of at home like refilling reusable water bottles. (Come to think of it, I envy the person who thought of putting ordinary water into plastic bottles for profit.) Consider significantly changing your lifestyle too. There are many measures you could take to do this, including downsizing your car or carpooling to save money on gas, buying groceries and making your meals at home instead of eating out, and selling possessions you don't need. Keep in mind, "Non-Recurring" expenses will fluctuate month to month. Sometimes these expenses will be higher if there is an emergency or your car breaks down. This is why it is important to have a healthy savings for accidentals as well as for large future purchases.

Car Loans

Now, not all debt is bad. Sometimes you may need help to buy that car. However, when negotiating to purchase a car, do not focus on the payment. Once when looking at cars, the dealer kept asking me what I wanted my monthly payment to be. Why should he care? Don't negotiate on the amount of a monthly payment; negotiate on the *total price* of the car. This is important because the dealer may lessen your monthly payments but extend the number of years it would take you to pay it off. Therefore, this is not a deal. They are taking advantage of your wallet, as you are paying more interest to the company and not reducing your total price. If you need direction on how to negotiate this, look back on the chapters that covered communication, negotiation, saying no, and decision-making.

Student Loans and Mortgages

You may be wondering about student loans. These days it is impossible to go through undergraduate or graduate school without incurring significant debt in student loans. Unfortunately, most creditors are vultures, taking advantage of the vulnerability and inexperience of young people. They encourage them to get student loans and student-plus loans without disclosing the fact that it may take a long time to pay these debts and that the accumulated interest might be astronomical. I advise people to only take out the minimum amount of student loans needed. Do not take out student loans and go on vacation. Make sure you are studying for a career that will enable you to pay off your student loans.

What about a mortgage to purchase a home? Very few people can buy a house without going through a bank. So, like student loans, a mortgage is a reasonable debt. Houses are a good investment because they tend to appreciate in value, giving you equity over time. In addition, owning a home and paying a mortgage tends to raise your credit score.

Cosigning

I have cosigned on loans twice in my life, and was seriously burnt in both cases. I was left responsible for the debt. Do not cosign. Bankers are not dummies. If the person asking you to cosign could afford it, the bankers would have already loaned them the money. So why would you want to take a risk that the bankers don't want to take? You may have a soft spot for your son, daughter, sister, or brother, but I strongly advise against cosigning. If you must, assume you are going to be the one paying the debt.

Credit Reports

In America, credit reports are issued by three agencies: Experian, Equifax, and TransUnion. They rate you with a number between 400 and 850. The higher the credit score, the more likely you will get approved for loans at a lower interest rate. This is one of the reasons that the rich are able to get richer and the poor tend to get poorer.

Focus on trying to increase your credit score. To do this you must pay your bills on time and keep your debt-to-earnings ratio within certain limits. There are also apps, such as myFICO, Credit.com, Lock &

Alert available from Equifax, Experian Boost, Transunion, ScoreSense, and Self that can help you increase your credit score by keeping you informed about the score and providing other advice.

Retirement

The average financial advisor will ask these questions: At what age do you want to retire? How do you want to live when retired? They will input these numbers into a software program and use the results to tell you how much you should be saving and how much you should be spending. I do not recommend this route. The idea of retirement suggests that you stop working, sit down by the beach in Florida (or some other warm spot), and drink beer or cocktails all day. We are not designed to be unproductive. The best response to a financial advisor who asks you this question is, "I never plan to retire." This always leaves them at a loss for words and gets them to leave you alone. Many studies done in England (where mandatory retirement exists) show that people who retire and do nothing suddenly become sick and drop dead. So why would you want to retire?

If you really need to talk to someone about some level of retirement planning, though, be sure to enlist the services of a recommended financial advisor with experience. They must consider much more than numbers; they should take into account your lifestyle, your goals, and who you want to be.

Insurance

Purchasing life insurance is a decision that can be life-saving for some families and poverty-inducing for others. I recommend getting a term life insurance. These tend to have lower rates. It would be better to save that money or invest it in mutual funds or real estate rather than life insurance. Whole life insurance has high premiums and these payments do not make a lot of sense. Instead, it would be smarter to invest the savings when choosing a term life insurance policy over a whole life insurance policy. However, if by divine means or a known health condition, you think you're not going to live long, it is worth having whole life insurance to provide for your family. Additionally, I do recommend that you get disability insurance before the age of forty-five since you never know what will happen in life.

Leaving a Legacy

Do you ever wonder why some families get rich from generation to generation and other families live in continued poverty instead? When you learn about finances and investment strategies, teach them to your children. They, in turn, will teach their children. This is an important method for passing wealth from one generation to the next. Consider this: Even if you make millions of dollars, you are eventually going to die and you can't take anything with you. What do you want people to say about you? Do you want them to say that you used your money to change lives? Do you want them to say you had twenty-five different Mercedes Benzes? Think about it. What do you want to leave behind? Doing this will help you decide what you do with your money. After all, your money is not truly yours; it belongs to the Lord. So live and leave a true and genuine legacy.

Section 3

Living a Balanced, Productive, and Fulfilling Life

Chapter 18: Emotional Well-Being

E motional well-being can be defined as the STET ability to adapt and cope in a positive manner when confronted with adverse life events. Your well-being is hugely significant and can affect your physical health and, ultimately, your outlook on life. A stable STET capacity to cope gives us the means to function properly in our personal relationships, at work, and through difficult life events without losing control.

Until recently, we didn't emphasize emotional well-being that much, but during and after the COVID pandemic, it was finally perceived as vitally important. As a result, mental health awareness has gained attention because people have suddenly recognized what social isolation can do. So one result of COVID was that we have learned to pay attention to our emotions.

Nobody can go through life without challenges, so it is important to know how to face them. *Psychological resilience* is positively correlated with emotional well-being. Psychological resilience is the ability to withstand negative life events without losing control.

There are many examples of psychological resilience around us. In my practice, I see many military veterans who have all been through the same war and all experienced trauma in it. Some of them are functioning well, and while they may have issues, they are employed and involved in personal relationships. However, others deal with issues that are much more difficult. They may develop substance abuse disorders or other maladaptive coping strategies. *Psychological resilience* is a term that differentiates between a person who is able to cope effectively versus one who cannot.

Emotional well-being is achieved when the focus is more on the positive than the negative of any situation. According to Franciscan friar and ecumenical teacher Father Richard Rohr, if we do not *transform* our pain, we will end up *transmitting* it. Unfortunately, it is likely to be transmitted to other people, like family members and coworkers. It can even be turned in on the person themselves in the form of a physical illness or acts of violence.

For example, during a period of employment at one healthcare institution, I worked with a person who constantly interfered with my work. This person came between me and my patients, gossiped about me, and repeatedly cost me time and effort. It continued for too long. As a result, many negative emotions arose within me, and I started to transmit these painful emotions toward my job at the institution.

Finally, I decided that I must forgive this person and free myself from this negativity reign of terror. This was not easy, but the ability to forgive helped me take control of my situation at work. I focused on how I was helping my patients rather than the other person's annoying behaviors. It took time, but I was able to put these workplace interactions into place. Through repeated efforts at forgiveness, I was able to reclaim my joy in my work. I quit transferring the triggered negative emotions onto other relationships, and they no longer affected my own psychological outlook. It was a process, but I am stronger for it.

Common Sources of Negative Emotions

The following situations and events may set off negative emotions. It is not an exhaustive list, but a guide to help you recognize what may trigger negative emotions for you.

- **Being under pressure:** I'm not a fan of multitasking. When I try to do too many things at once, I make mistakes. Because I am making mistakes, I feel overwhelmed and anxious about those mistakes. Ultimately, the tasks end up taking *more* time, rather than less, because I have to correct my mistakes. When I am under pressure and simultaneously fixing my mistakes, I just make even more mistakes. So, as much as possible, one should avoid being under too much pressure.

- **Not feeling appreciated:** Not feeling valued can lead to resentment. Employers should especially be aware of this. Recognize when employees do well and give them honest appreciation. If you are in a situation in which you do not feel valued, you need to review that role and seek advice about how to handle it in an emotionally healthy manner.

- **Lack of control**: Feeling that you don't have control when you are responsible for something is stressful. For example, there are some institutions where physicians are legally responsible for the actions of coworkers over whom they have no control. You may be asked to sign off on the notes of a nurse practitioner or physician assistant whom you have not spoken to or supervised. Because of your position, you are asked to sign these notes. Personally, I will not do this. There is a danger of lawsuits, and it is too emotionally stressful.

- **Discrimination**: If you are judged because of your sex, religious beliefs, color, or anything at all, it can be a source of negative emotions.

- **Hatred:** Experiencing hate causes stress. This includes dealing with the unkindness of other people and being bullied.

- **Big transitions:** All kinds of big decisions and changes are potential sources of negative emotions and stress. These include buying a home, getting married, going through a divorce, mourning the death of a loved one, or maintaining difficult but necessary relationships. Additionally, there's the day-to-day and as well as unanticipated stresses of life: exhaustion and hunger, working long hours consistently without breaks, periods of unemployment, taking care of sick family members, living through natural disasters, and many other instances.

How to Recognize Negative Emotions

While you should recognize *all* your emotions, it is especially important to recognize the negative ones. An initial negative emotion can take several different forms, such as:

- Anger
- Fear
- Anxiety
- Frustration
- Jealousy
- Hatred
- Sadness
- Guilt
- Depression

Additionally, negative emotions can manifest as secondary emotions and actions. Extreme examples include lashing out and physical abuse. Fear can lead to demonizing others. For example, the fear that immigrants will displace workers has led to their mistreatment and violence against them. In general, secondary emotions may present themselves as physical symptoms that can come into play, including:

- Dizziness
- Lack of focus
- Chest pain
- Rapid heart rate
- Nausea
- Vomiting
- Irritable Bowel Syndrome (IBS)

Secondary emotions and physical symptoms signal that there is something going on in the background. When these are present, you must go back and figure out what's really going on inside and analyze the source of your initial negative feelings.

The following strategy can be used to identify triggers or sources of negative emotions. Ask yourself:

1. What am I feeling now? Am I feeling frightened, sad, angry, jealous, nauseated, dizzy?

2. Have I felt this before? If so, in what circumstances? (This can be compared to a postmortem—have I felt this before?) What happened in the past when I felt like this?

3. What events led me to feeling like this now? Can I correlate it with the past?

4. Sometimes during the first attempt, you can't identify the source. Keep going over the questions and often the answer will come.

This process can be hard, especially if it involves a repressed memory or event. If you decided to suppress it, it becomes more difficult to bring out, because the mind does not want to release it. The mind has blocked the emotions associated with bringing it out. In these cases, we can be intellectually doing the exercises, but there is a strong degree of suppression making it difficult to release.

I experienced the beneficial results of releasing suppressed emotions when I went to see a psychologist who did experiential treatments. She helped me reenact things from the past that were forgotten, repressed, or suppressed. My appointment with her for this experiential session occurred before a weekend. What happened during the next three nights surprised me. When I went to bed, I had a lot of physical pain all night. This pain didn't resolve with anti-inflammatories and lasted all night for three nights.

My mind had been suppressing all these negative emotions. When she helped me bring them out, it resulted in physical pain, but this was a good thing! Those emotions left the subconscious and manifested physically for a short period of time. They manifested as general physical pain instead of lack of sleep, high blood pressure, stomach problems, or back pain. Those suppressed emotions came out and were released. In the end, I felt much better.

Managing Negative Emotions

I have examined some common sources of negative emotions and how to recognize when secondary emotions are operating within us, and I have offered a strategy to help identify initial negative emotions, secondary emotions, and emotional triggers. The next step is to learn how to manage these emotions so you can adapt and cope with situations and events more positively. Management strategies are key to helping us unlock every negative emotion and support our emotional well-being.

Forgive when you are offended. This is the big one. As mentioned before, refusing to forgive is like drinking poison and hoping the other person dies. Forgiveness is not a feeling, but a choice. Sometimes you need to forgive several times. It's a process that can occur again and again. However, continuing to do it is good. It brings healing and restores hope. It's important to remember that forgiveness is not forgetting. Forgetting may allow the same offense to take place again, which causes unnecessary damage. You can remember and still forgive.

Change your thoughts! If your emotion takes the form of a negative thought, you can change it or replace it. For example, if a negative emotion tells you that you are a worthless nobody, take the time to go back and look at the good things you have in your life. Actively change your thought to reflect those good things. Say to yourself, "I am worthy and valuable," and keep repeating that until you believe it.

Move! Get up and get dressed. Take a walk. Dance. Go to the gym. Stretch. Physical movement has a tremendous effect on your ability to deal with negative emotions. Especially dancing!

Make changes by adopting some kind of new action. Do something you have never done before. Try a different activity. Explore a hobby, like gardening or fishing. Delve into unfamiliar territories. Be open to things you haven't done before. Try something new. Connect with your community and surround yourself with positive people. Join a club or a small group at church.

Find altruistic pastimes. Taking actions that benefit others is a powerful way to deal with negative emotions. Overcome evil with good. Do good—either to the person who hurt you or to society. Feed the homeless, make a donation, give alms. Be extra kind to people—as in everyone, including yourself! All of this helps you be more kind to yourself and ultimately happier.

Unfortunately, many people don't recognize the power of doing good and might be motivated to do the opposite instead. They might think, *This person has treated me wrongly, so I am going to get him back by doing this or that.* They are now stuck in a cycle of negativity. That doesn't work. Neither does making poor choices for yourself, such as drinking too much or otherwise disrespecting yourself. Intentionally choosing to act kindly toward yourself and others can go a long way in the healing process all around.

Sleep and rest. Be sure to get adequate sleep at night. Take time for extra relaxation. Don't live your life frantically chasing deadlines and in a hurry. Slow down.

Treat yourself well. Schedule positive self-care, such as massages, pedicures, manicures, or shopping for new clothing. Take time out in nature. Do what is important to you.

Confront when necessary. Sometimes you may need to gently confront a person who may be triggering difficult emotions. Do this in a logical way, without intense emotions, as outlined in the chapter on conflict resolution.

More About Negative Emotions

Negative emotions are not all that bad! Sometimes they are an important signal to you. This is a potential advantage. The signal might be telling you that something big is on the line or alerting you about something that is wrong. For example, sadness can be a signal of major depression; this signal can help you realize that there is something going on in your brain. Mild anxiety can actually make you more productive, so that's not always bad. It depends on the amount of anxiety you are experiencing. Anger can be a signal that something is going on in the background and can help you figure out how to deal with it. Guilt can be a motivation to change your behavior for the better. So please remember, negative emotions are not always bad. They may work to your advantage.

Overall, however, you must govern your thoughts with care because they influence who you truly are. The following quote is widely attributed to a mystic philosopher of ancient China named Lao Tzu, best known as the author of the *Tao Te Ching*. It's has been credited to many other people, but Lao Tzu is the earliest.

"Watch your thoughts, they become your words;
watch your words, they become your actions;
watch your actions, they become your habits;
watch your habits, they become your character;
watch your character, it becomes your destiny."

Chapter 19: Boundaries

Boundaries are defined as a dividing line or barrier that separates us from another person. In this context, I will discuss boundaries as they relate to persons rather than properties. We will primarily focus on boundaries at work, but these principles also apply to the importance of good boundaries in marriage, with our children and friends, and in our social lives.

Let's start with a few stories to help illustrate the concept of boundaries.

The Language of Flowers

During my residency, one of my male colleagues, a good psychiatrist, had a female patient who was hospitalized. When patients are in the hospital, we usually perform courtesy visits. This is a nice thing to do. My colleague brought flowers when he visited this patient. However, this led to the patient romanticizing the relationship, and, unfortunately, in her mind it stopped being a doctor-patient relationship. She started thinking that something big might come of a romantic relationship with my colleague. She became delusional and obsessed, so much so that he had to terminate his professional relationship with the patient.

I know about this because the patient was referred to me. For about two years I treated this patient, and she remained convinced that my colleague was in love with her and that he was going to leave his wife and come to her. I was unable to shake her delusion.

This psychiatrist broke a boundary. His intention was harmless, but he shouldn't have given flowers to this patient. She interpreted the flowers as a romantic gesture between a man and a woman, not the meaning my colleague attributed to bringing those flowers to a hospital patient. This story also shows that if you don't communicate boundaries clearly, there can be misinterpretations.

Check Your Assumptions

During my medical training, I was advised to say yes to every responsibility. The assumption behind this advice was, *You are a foreigner in this land. You are black. You are competing in a white man's world, so you cannot do the same things your colleagues are doing. You have to work five, even six times as hard as they do.* This was communicated to me and, unfortunately, I have communicated the same to other people in the past.

As a result, I took on everything. I volunteered for everything. Someone asked, "Who wants to do this?" I did. Over time, my colleagues and supervisors got used to this. Then one day, I was unable to go to a meeting because my son was sick. I chose to be with my son. Then, the hundreds of voluntary actions I previously performed were instantly forgotten. This one time I said "no" was identified and commented on by my boss during my evaluation. He said, "We needed you to attend this meeting and you didn't do it."

I learned from this experience that I wasn't being careful about creating boundaries between what I could do and what I could not do. I was giving them the impression that they could do whatever they wanted with my time. I was being taken for granted. After that, I was careful about what I agreed to do. I did not instantly volunteer. Instead, I said, "Let me think about it." In this way, I bought myself time. Later on, I decided that I would not volunteer extra services. Only if they really needed me, I would then volunteer my services. That worked well because I was then seen as a hero in the situation. Even though I was working significantly less, the perception was that I was saving the day. Isn't that ironic?

Boundaries are very important because they protect our energy and values, as well as our health and wellness. When we lack clear boundaries, it can lead to feelings of being unappreciated. That's how I felt during that evaluation: burned out, undervalued, and disrespected.

Types of Boundaries

There are several types of boundaries that help us survive and thrive throughout our lives. They're everywhere. Here's a list of the general ones followed by the workplace ones in their own section.

- **Physical boundaries:** Everyone has boundaries governing physical touch. This may also include food and drink preferences.
- **Emotional boundaries:** How much of my emotional self do I want to share with somebody else? And who do I choose to share my emotions with? For example, do you want to share your emotional life on social media? Emotional boundaries are necessary for our well-being. I remember a colleague who stopped an ex-boyfriend from calling and speaking to her abusively. She finally said, "If you continue to talk like that, I am going to stop this phone call and block you." When he continued to call, she blocked his access. This emotional boundary was very powerful and an act of both self-care and self-respect.
- **Time boundaries:** Most of us do not handle this one very well. An example of a time boundary is when I promise somebody I'll be there by noon, but don't show up until 12:30 p.m. When this happens, I am not being respectful of the other person's time. On the other side, though, if the other person decides to entertain me when I am thirty minutes late, it shows their lack of straightfor-

ward boundaries. If I have patients scheduled at 12:00 p.m., and they show up forty-five minutes late and I still see them, I am not respecting my own boundaries. There's also a strong chance I'm going to eat into the time of the next several patients. When I allow this to happen, the next person is shortchanged, and it can go on and on like that. There are also social and cultural boundaries regarding time to keep in mind. When people aren't familiar with social norms, they can be surprised or hurt by some situations. For example, in Nigeria it is an unwritten rule that you must be late to a party. Someone new to that culture may be hurt and surprised when no one shows up to their party on time!

- **Relational boundaries:** It is vital to have clear communication around the expectations in a relationship. One obvious example is in obtaining clear consent when relationships become sexual, but there are many others. Relationships are work.

- **Intellectual boundaries:** Make sure to protect a new discovery, patent process, or original work from theft. Additionally, do not steal other people's work! Social media and the internet complicate these boundaries. For example, my son created a series of short videos on social media that used scenarios and characters from anime to help illustrate the meanings behind some Bible stories and Christian teachings. Later he found that another person used the same examples and concepts for their own video series, which was also published on social media. In this scenario, my son learned the lesson that sharing things on the internet can be stolen by others. He emotionally recovered, but this is a small example of what can happen if you are not careful with your intellectual property.

Workplace Boundaries

Pay special attention to workplace boundaries, because we spend a lot of time at work, sometimes eight or more hours in a twenty-four-hour day. That is thirty-three percent of our lives! If you live to one hundred, that is thirty-three years of your life.

Many people do not understand why it is important to set workplace boundaries, so when explaining your need for workplace boundaries to employers and coworkers, some good ways to phrase this might be:

- "For my own emotional wellness, this is what I can take, and this is what I cannot take."
- "You are actually helping me be more productive if you agree to my boundaries."
- "I know myself more than you know me—I know what I can take and what I cannot take. So, at the end of the day this is going to be good for you, because I'm not going to burn out."

Unfortunately, the consequences of not having workplace boundaries include:

- Tiredness
- Anxiety
- Depression
- Forgetfulness
- Irritability
- Physical problems (such as gastrointestinal problems, headaches, joint pains, back pains, and more)

I've had people tell me that on a Monday morning, they don't want to go to work and start feeling sick; while on Saturdays, since they are not going to work because it is the weekend, they feel better. In this scenario the correct treatment is not necessarily antidepressants. Or perhaps they should gently confront their employer to find out if they are willing to make changes. If your employer will not work to change the situation or respect boundaries, you have to make a change and get another job.

When workplace boundaries are not clearly erected and maintained, there is a higher risk that work and workplace problems will spill into your personal life, which can affect relationships with your spouse, friends, parents, and children. The best strategy is to become aware of your own vulnerability. If you have difficulty setting boundaries or sticking to those boundaries, it's best to know this about yourself. If you don't realize what you are doing, as happened to me in the past when I felt that I had to prove myself by working harder than my colleagues, you will experience burnout. Know yourself enough to say, "When it comes to work, I like boundaries, but I have trouble sticking to them." That's a good first step to addressing the problems. It's best to set boundaries *before* you start to burn out, but nevertheless, when you sense burnout approaching, there is still time to establish boundaries and help yourself.

How to Set Up Workplace Boundaries

Here are several examples and strategies for setting workplace boundaries.

- **Don't stay after your scheduled work time unless it is absolutely necessary.** Use a balanced approach. Being a good worker doesn't mean you regularly stay past your scheduled work hours. If the end of your shift is 5 p.m., you can decide to stay five to ten minutes later once in a while, but if you stay until 6 p.m. every day, there is something wrong. One strategy that helps with this is to refrain from responding to text messages and emails outside your normal work hours. Keep them silenced during vacations. Sending emails should be done within certain reasonable times. You should not send emails or respond to them at awkward hours. For example, I don't want to be responding to emails at 3 a.m. Once my boss sent an email to me at 9:01 a.m. I knew that the subject of the email had been on his mind all night, but he waited until 9:01 to send it. This is the proper way to handle work communication. Remember, it's up to you, the employee, to keep from getting trapped in demands outside of scheduled work hours. Don't say yes to the things you don't have to do. Use the tactic, "Let me think about it. Let me check with my family." This strategy works well for me.

- **Do not work on unscheduled weekends and during vacation times.** Definitely do not work on your days off or weekends. If you are working extra hours, be sure to be paid for the extra time. Beware of workplaces that want to give you a laptop. This might trick you into performing work tasks during unpaid hours.

- **Take frequent breaks.** It has become common for people to work through their lunch hour and not take breaks. The breaks are in your schedule for a reason, and if you are not taking them, you are missing out on time to relax and refresh, which would ultimately make you more productive.

- **If you work from home, designate your work space that is set apart from your living space.** This helps you psychologically know when you are working. When you are in the designated space, you are working, and when you are not in the designated work space, you are relaxing. This helps you keep a boundary of separation so that your work and home life do not get meshed together.

- **Use your vacation time, paid time off, sick time, and mental health days.** This is time you are getting paid for, and is part of your benefits. You are entitled to it and should use it as such.

- **Turn down tasks that are not in your job description.** If you are an administrative assistant, your boss shouldn't be sending you to pick up the dry cleaning.

- **Delegate and allocate tasks.** For example, if I need papers shredded and office staff are nearby, I ask them to do it. That's one less thing that I have to do, and it is part of their job description.

- **Do not overdo overtime.** This kind of pay can be useful to pay off some bills now and then, but it's called overtime for a reason. It is *over the time* you are supposed to work. If you constantly work overtime hours, you will get into trouble and will burn out.

Communicating Your Boundaries

Now that we know how to set boundaries, let's discuss communicating them to your employer. It's one thing to know what you want and need, but what are the best ways to approach the employer? There are three steps to follow:

1. **Recognition.** The lack of boundaries can affect your emotional and physical health, your relationships, and even your commitment to your job. Understand within yourself that the situation is not good, and that it is not working.

2. **Decide on which boundaries to set.** Ask yourself, *What are my boundaries regarding this issue?*

3. **Communicate these boundaries in a very clear and succinct way.** Keep emotions out of it. Make sure your message is not personal and stays factual. You want to be clearly understood. Dropping a hint or wishing that your employer would know your boundaries is not going to work. You have to talk about it. I recommend having an initial verbal conversation, followed by a written communication. Send a note along the lines of, "As we discussed yesterday, this is what I want to see going forward regarding my time." You want the communication in writing. This will reinforce your message.

Be ready for pushback, but stick to your guns. If you cave in, you've lost a good opportunity to address your emotional wellness. Your employer, or others in your life, will be less likely to take you seriously when you try to set boundaries a second time. You can also use any pushback as an opportunity to re-communicate your boundaries more clearly.

Summary

Boundaries are useful and important in almost every aspect of our lives. When it comes to leadership, all of the types of boundaries discussed in this chapter are relevant. Keep these lessons on boundaries in mind as we approach leadership styles and skills in the next chapter. Boundary setting is necessary for groups to work together successfully, and those engaged in leading must also establish limits on their physical, emotional, relational, and intellectual expectations others may have. The ability to set boundaries is an important element within effective leadership.

Chapter 20: Leadership and Leadership Skills

A leader is someone who can effect change in positive or negative ways. Adolf Hitler was a leader with many followers, and he brought about great evil. Nelson Mandela was also a leader, but his actions brought about great good. These two examples show that there is no consistent playbook for being an effective leader.

Some people have natural talents and skills to effectively lead, while others have to work and develop them. This chapter will not discuss the details of leadership, but rather provide a synopsis or overview of leadership. It will help you recognize the kinds of leaders for whom you prefer to work, as well as your own style of leadership. If you want to know more and get into more detail, there are books and training available, such as those provided by Townsend Leadership Development Coaching. My wife and I have been to one of these conferences, and it was very good. That's just one of the many options out there. There are many others.

Leadership Styles

There are several leadership styles. Most people choose a leadership style that fits their personality, experience, and/or background. Knowing what works for you as a leader is a very important part of becoming a good leader. For example, if my personality is not authoritarian, it is not going to be effective for me to try to lead with authoritarian methods. Since that's not the way I think, it would not work for me.

Here are seven basic types of leadership styles. Read over them and decide which one best fits your leadership pattern. However, understand that these styles are not exclusive of one another; they often overlap, so one person may have traits across many leadership styles. Personally, I have some traits of both democratic and coaching leadership styles. Others may have none of these traits, in which case they may have to create their own leadership style, or it could be that they were not born to lead.

Autocratic (or Authoritarian) Leadership

As Americans, we do not like these words because they stand against the essence of freedom. However, autocratic or authoritarian leadership can be effective in some situations. An autocratic leader has very clear visions and goals. They have specific guidelines with no room for collaboration or negotiation. This type of leadership can be effective when there is no time for discussion, or when a decision is needed immediately to prevent dire consequences. A good example is the role of a military commander in wartime. When the military commander directs troops to retreat, there is no argument. There is no time to convince the troops that they should retreat because harm may come to them. A surgeon in the operating room is another good example. If a patient is bleeding, the surgeon must be decisive and tell the assistants what to do. It is an emergency situation.

The downside of this leadership style is in its potential for abuse, as we have seen with military dictators all over the world. In the workplace environment, an autocratic boss may use tactics such as changing the schedule for their employees without telling them. Authoritarian leaders also decrease or diminish creativity in the people around them. Employees often don't feel heard or appreciated with this leadership style, which may cause friction and stress.

Pacesetting Leadership

We worked on a project in Kenya recently with a leader who exhibited this leadership style. A pacesetting leader pushes their team to run hard and fast to the finish line. They lead by example, setting high expectations and carrying the team along. Unlike the autocratic person who dictates the actions of those underneath them, the pace setter is part of the group. You are all in it together. The pace is quick, the vision is clear, and you go together. This style works for highly motivated employees and works well if you have a deadline.

For example, in Kenya we had ten days, we knew what we had to achieve, and we knew how to do it. The leader wasn't sitting down drinking coffee and telling us what to do; we were doing it together. Goals are achieved in a timely manner with this kind of leadership, but the team can feel burnt out. It's hard to sustain this kind of energy for significant amounts of time. We couldn't have worked in Kenya like that for ninety days.

Transformational Leadership

My wife displays this kind of leadership style. These are visionary leaders. They are committed and have a strong image of their goal within themselves. Their goal and vision is their source of inspiration. From it, they focus on their vision and use it to energize their team. This style is especially effective when people need direction. Some organizations lack direction and goals, so a transformational leader can come in with the big vision and use motivation and inspiration to energize the organization. The downside of this type of leadership is that it may lack practicality. Transformational leaders do not always consider what it takes to accomplish their vision and might ignore daily tasks. This leadership is good if the resources are there, and if there is no direction, a transformational leader can supply the needed motivation to realize the vision. However, if the resources are not there, you can have the vision, but it won't happen anyway.

Coaching Leadership

A coaching leader sees unexplored potential in the team they lead. They tap into the individuality, uniqueness, and resources of their team. They use regular feedback, which is generally positive, but also constructive, to nurture their team's strengths. This style is effective when there is time to devote to the project. It is good for teambuilding groups that are open to change. Coaching leaders boost the morale of the team and usually create a positive work atmosphere. However, this style can't work if there's not enough time and can't work in an emergency. You can't wait for coaching when someone is bleeding. This leadership style works best if there is enough time and there are unique potentials in the people and situations that haven't been tapped. It doesn't work for team members who are lazy, don't pull their weight, or resist being part of a team.

Democratic Leadership

A democratic leader seeks and gains the team's input before making decisions. The goal is to listen to everyone's input, although the leader still has the final say. The team must be able to speak up, otherwise there will be no input. The advantage to this type of leadership is that it gives all team members a voice and can help build trust. It also fosters creativity. Unfortunately, if there isn't enough time for all that, it doesn't work and can result in prolonged decision-making. In fact, the decisions may never be made.

Facilitative Leadership

When I am part of a group, I like this style. This leader puts the team first and pays attention to their emotional and professional needs. Decisions are left to the team. The facilitative leader uses praise and encouragement to build up the team. This is effective when morale is low, there is conflict among the team members, or even when there is a degree of high stress. Each person's well-being is a priority and conflict is resolved more effectively with this leader because the team members can see that the leader values their opinion. The downside is that individual needs are overshadowed. Additionally, using facilitative leadership techniques on a project or business with the focus on what everybody wants may sacrifice what is best for the company. There can be a delay in getting to the goal. However, when facilitative (and the upcoming delegative) leadership styles are used with highly competent people (those who are already solid and don't need coaching), the work gets done. All you need to do is give the team the project and guide them, and you help them work out any conflicts they have among themselves. This is a common leadership style in academics. Since most of the team members are high achievers, the leader wants to guide and encourage them toward achieving organizational goals without being heavy-handed.

Delegative or Laissez-faire Leadership

This style allows the team to work out issues among themselves with minimum guidance. The leader is passive. This is effective when you have highly qualified team members with strong track records. It's also effective when you need "out of the box" thinking, and when you need to tap into the creativity of people with accomplished backgrounds and history. The leader is not involved in day-to-day issues. A downside to this leadership style is that it also allows significant disagreements. Often everyone on the team is a specialist. Delegative leadership is not useful when the team members are not highly qualified or well-trained.

Effective Leadership

Whatever your leadership style, use the right style for the situation. Flexibility is necessary if you want to be effective. Here's a list of common themes that everyone needs in order to practice effective leadership:

- Clear vision and purpose.

- Constant and regular communication with the team. (If there is no communication, people presume and assume what should be done.)
- Empathy and appreciation shown to team members. (This helps give them a sense of belonging.)
- Flexible strategies. Flexible strategies with a willingness to change, along with having clear goals and vision, is the key to success.
- Ability to move toward difficult situations. Leadership coach and psychologist John Townsend teaches that the natural tendency of human beings is to avoid something difficult, but an effective leader moves *toward* difficult situations and finds ways to solve them.
- Taking risks, but not recklessly.
- Multigenerational and multiethnic understanding. The world is getting smaller and we all need multicultural ways of thinking to solve problems and effect positive change.
- Vulnerability and transparency. It helps for team members to see the leader as a human being, but you must be careful about sharing too much; there has to be a balance and healthy and clear boundaries in place.

Developing Your Own Style

Now that we have discussed different leadership styles and we have a sense of the traits necessary for successful leadership, you can develop your own style. Keep the following points in mind.

- **Know yourself.** Do you prefer to give orders, delegate, or receive input? In other words, are you a hands-on or hands-off person? Knowing this will help you identify your style and develop it further.
- **Know your team.** Are you leading highly qualified people? In that case, you don't need to use the coaching style because they don't require coaching. Instead, you should use either a

laissez-faire or democratic style of leadership. However, if your team requires inspiration (and you have the time for it), coaching is a better choice. Learn from previous mistakes. If you try a style that is not compatible with the people on your team, then be willing to change it.

How we live our lives and the impact we have on people and projects can last beyond our lifetime. It's worth considering how to pass on the fruits of your learning and labors to benefit future generations. The next chapter discusses the concept of legacy.

Chapter 21: Legacy

The young and ambitious do not think much about their legacy. Their focus is on what they want to achieve, who they want to marry, how much money they want to make, and how many houses they want to own. However, as people grow older, they recognize they are not invincible. That's when you start to think about what happens when you're gone. The question of legacy becomes much more important. It's a time to reassess your values. After you are gone from this world, what part of you will continue to live?

For the past several years, I have asked my students this question: "What do you want people to say about you at your funeral?" I ask this question, not because I want to be negative, but because I want them to start thinking about their legacy at a younger age.

Leaving a legacy is a way to make an impact that will last for generations. Think about somebody you've never met, but who you think you know very well. That person may have done something that is of value and importance to you. Common examples of well-known people who have left excellent legacies are Mother Theresa, Queen Elizabeth II, Abraham Lincoln, Nelson Mandela, and Mahatma Gandhi.

A legacy goes beyond the things you do for yourself. It can refer to what you say about yourself or what people say about you. The latter is much more powerful than the former. If you're wondering why you even have to leave a legacy, the answer is, of course, you don't. That's your choice. But why *not* leave a legacy? A legacy does not have to be financial, and you don't have to be a world leader or the richest person in order to leave one. Let's discuss several types of legacies that we can leave behind.

How to Leave a Legacy

The first thing you want to consider is the impact others have had on your life. My father was one of the most selfless people I have ever met. As a boy, when we ate our dinner, he never finished his food. Once I asked him, "Why don't you finish your food?" He responded, "You have to think of others." In my boyhood home, we had a maid, household staff, and cooks. Even though the staff had their own food (what my father was served was top-notch), he always saved some for them. This simple act that I observed as a boy left a lifelong impact on me.

The second consideration is knowing your purpose and values and being in touch with your passion in life. Understanding these will help guide you in conceiving your legacy. An excellent discovery tool is writing your own obituary. Imagine that the time has come, and you are gone. People are coming to your funeral. You have the chance to write what people are going to be saying. There may be some experiences and lessons from your life that you would like to share. It helps to know what your priorities are. The act of writing your obituary can help you start thinking about how you still have the rest of your life to make changes. Perhaps by making changes, you can control what people will say about you when you die. It will also help you clearly see what you have already built in your life.

The main questions to help you consider leaving a legacy are:

- What would you want people to know about you?
- What is unique about you?

- Who has influenced your life?
- In what ways have others had a memorable impact on your life?

Legacy Examples

Forge a family tradition. About four years ago, my wife suggested that we should be breaking bread, or taking communion, with our children every Sunday. Communion is a tradition among Christians that symbolizes the acceptance of Jesus' sacrifice for us. During communion, we take crackers and grape juice to remember His love for us. So around seven o'clock in the evening we Facetime one another and there are usually three families represented. Once on the phone, we talk about the events from the week, then we take communion, pray, and continue to talk for a little while longer. We rarely miss a week! Even when we are traveling, our grown children will text us, asking, "When are we going to break bread?" They live in different parts of the U.S., so this is all long-distance. Part of the motivation on our part was to keep in contact with our family, our children, and it has become a healthy tradition to pass on. This tradition is helping us create a legacy, which is represented by our family connection, showing concern, expressing love, and emphasizing the importance of seeing and talking to each other.

Write a Book!

Rather than allowing other people to write about you, you can write your own biography. Leave a narrative for your children's children. That's a legacy that can go on for generations. My wife's father did this. The grandchildren and great-grandchildren read it to this day and are able to find out about their ancestor.

Be Generous

Generous people touch many lives and leave a snowball of a legacy. It doesn't take a lot of money to be generous. You could leave part of a 401K retirement fund to a charitable or beneficial organization. It doesn't have to be a five-million-dollar donation; it could be a couple hundred dollars that somebody, perhaps a homeless person, can use to get back on their feet. There are so many things you can do that will keep your legacy going and going. You can use the interest from a bank account to help others. Interest of fifty dollars a month could feed hungry people around the world. These gifts touch many lives.

Trust Funds

Set up a trust fund for a cause that is dear to your heart. You can also include a clause in your will. Dedicate a percentage of your estate to a cause that will continue to live after you die. Leave part of your property to a women's or homeless shelter. My mother-in-law, who's still alive, decided to leave her house to her church. When we she passes, her home will be used to house visiting pastors or missionaries. This is a selfless and altruistic decision that will benefit many in her memory. Her family knows about it, so there will be no fighting. That's leaving a legacy: thinking of others, not just yourself or your immediate family.

Think About It!

Since we spend a lot of our life at work, who wants that to be their only legacy? By developing character and values, prioritizing family time, and helping to build community, people contribute their gifts in many different ways. Financial legacies help those you leave behind and are just one way to honor your life's work and your family heritage. Take the time to really think about what you want to leave behind you, and intentionally choose to put whatever is needed in place in your life so that you can do it. Then your legacy will bless the generations that follow.

Meet the Author

Kola Alao, MD is a psychiatrist who lives and works in New York State. Growing up in Western Nigeria, he first moved to the United Kingdom, and then the United States, for advanced medical training. Experience as an immigrant has given him fresh insights on human behavior. Teaching medical students and residents has further expanded his familiarity with motivation and the drive for achievement. Dr. Alao writes from a deep understanding of human psychology combined with years of thorough, genuine self-reflection.

Dedicated to living his values as a Christian, husband, father, and medical doctor, he always sees the good in other people, turning a compassionate eye on each person's effort to improve themselves, encouraging everyone to make positive changes that align with their values, behaviors, and aspirations. Introducing tried-and-true methods to track the habits and character flaws that hold people back, Dr. Alao asks his readers to look deep within and offers his help.

With years of experience practicing a variety of therapeutic methods, Dr. Alao and his wife, a psychiatric nurse practitioner, have developed helpful treatments for depression, post-traumatic stress disorder, obsessive compulsive behaviors, and substance abuse disorders utilizing transcranial magnetic stimulation (TMS). They are active in their church and also spend considerable time each year volunteering with orphans and other populations in several African countries.

In this book, Dr. Alao shares his insights and wisdom with those who seek to build successful lives, offering good advice to help us make meaningful contributions to our communities and the wider world. Dr. Kola Alao can be contacted at 360favor@gmail.com or by visiting www.tmspsychiatry.org.